The Truce of God

The Truce of God

Rowan Williams

With a Foreword by
Robert Cantuar
former Archbishop of Canterbury

William B. Eerdmans Publishing Company
Grand Rapids, Michigan / Cambridge, U.K.

First published 1983 by Fount Paperbacks, London,
in association with Faith Press

This edition published 2005 by
Wm. B. Eerdmans Publishing Co.
255 Jefferson Ave. S.E., Grand Rapids, Michigan 49503 /
P.O. Box 163, Cambridge CB3 9PU U.K.

Printed in the United States of America

10 09 08 07 06 05   7 6 5 4 3 2 1

ISBN 0-8028-2790-X

www.eerdmans.com

Contents

Foreword

Nobody would deny that the search for peace in the world is one of mankind's most important tasks. Our Lord said 'Blessed are the peace makers' and his followers cannot justify the name of Christian unless they share his passion for peace.

The subject, however, is commonly overlaid with bland consensus clichés and the kind of pious rhetoric which has a bewildering and depressing effect even upon the best-intentioned. The merit of Rowan Williams' new book *The Truce of God* is that it probes behind words like 'reconciliation' which we use too easily, to reveal the profound realism of the way in which the concepts of peace and violence have been understood in the Bible and in later Christian tradition.

Although the author is a distinguished young theologian working in a university, his book is not academic in the pejorative sense. It is fresh and contemporary in its language and illustrations, and organized in such a way that it would provide an excellent and creatively controversial basis for a Lent study group.

The Truce of God is an enemy to easy illusions and a sign that

the Christian faith has the potential to make a unique contribution to peace-making. I hope that it will be widely studied.

Lambeth Palace   ROBERT CANTUAR
November 1982

Introduction

Anyone picking up a Lent Book and finding its opening pages mostly concerned with the world of popular fantasy and fiction might be forgiven for feeling some bewilderment; so a brief word of explanation may be in order. When I was invited to begin work on this book, I felt an urgent need to move away a little from the normal patterns of this sort of literature and see what it might be like to approach questions about Christian life and prayer in the context of a highly specific set of contemporary concerns — asking, in effect, what is the good news for *this* situation?

Such an approach is full of potential pitfalls. You can so define the 'contemporary concerns' that the Gospel fits neatly into the place you have already cleared for it; you can trivialize the Gospel by binding it to the passing trends of secular interest. I expect this book will be accused of both failings, and I am aware that it is unlikely to have avoided these traps entirely. But I cannot believe that the effort is misplaced. An essay in Christian spirituality written in the 1980s which completely ignored the collective neuroses of our society would be dishonest and destructive: it would imply that 'spirituality' was *not* about the learning of a particular kind of human life, open-eyed, responsive and candid. And because a great part of our collective neurosis seems to me to be rooted in certain sorts of fear, with their consequent refusal to see, I have chosen to come at the question of what it is like now to live and pray Christianly by way of looking at our fears and their slow corruption of our imagination. So that the goal of a book like this one is something to do with a salutary shock to the imagination and a rebirth of its proper critical and hopeful dimensions.

I have written about peace, internal and external. I make no secret of the fact that I have strong convictions about the way forward to a more peaceful and less threatened world, convictions which I hold in common with a growing number of Christian people, including the authors of the Anglican report on *The Church and the Bomb*, which appeared when this book was at proof stage. Obviously I run the risk of having this volume dismissed as partisan or propagandist by those who think that any expression of opinion on this subject by Christians is some sort of compromising of the non-political purity of the Gospel. But it is not meant as a propaganda exercise on behalf of one kind of political solution. Many will disagree with my response to the problem: my hope, though, is that some agreement may be possible about the *nature* of the problem and its theological and spiritual dimensions. With this in mind, I have tried to concentrate on this latter area rather than on the vexed questions of practical policy making.

A lot of what I have written owes a great debt to the work of Thomas Merton, and I can say that this book is, in some sense, written in his honour and for his memory. But I have also to acknowledge all those living friends and teachers who have shared their wisdom with me — Professor Donald Mackinnon above all, and many Christian acquaintances in Cambridge over the past few years: Jim Garrison, Roger Paul, Alan Smith, Peter Tamplin, and others engaged in the cause of peace and in discussing the Christian issues involved. This book would be duller and shallower without them. And lastly, my warm thanks to the Archbishop of Canterbury for encouraging the writing of this work and for providing a foreword: his generous support has helped enormously.

R.W.

The Truce of God

1 Fears and Fantasies

There is no shortage of people to complain that ours is a society obsessed with violence. But by 'violence', such people usually mean not much more than the level of realism with which physical struggle and physical injury are shown on television and cinema screens; analysis of the context and the character of this surface violence seems less forthcoming. Yet it is an analysis badly needed. There is nothing much new about the realities of struggle and injury, and long before an advanced special effects technology made film representation of this so much more appallingly convincing, explicit verbal description was perfectly possible and not at all rare. It may well be that the level of realism we now tolerate in visual representations of violence means that our imaginations are becoming significantly brutalized or insensitive: I think this is probably so, and it is worrying, but it isn't the main point I want to make at the moment.

What is new, and what does need analysis, is the kind of violence which seems to have swamped enormous areas of the popular market, especially in the cinema and in cheap paperback fiction. It is not easy to characterize it in a nutshell; but I suppose its main feature could be seen as a quality of utter uncontrollability and unpredictability quite removed from the human scale and from the sphere of normal human interaction. One form of this is the 'catastrophe' fantasy based on the malfunctioning or collapse of some bit of the rather threatening world of complex technology — the aircraft disaster, the burning tower block, the chemical leak. Out of the vague sense most of us have, that in a sophisticated technology there are countless things that just might go wrong on an enormous scale, fantasy generates the details for a disaster story. And perhaps the most important aspect of this process is the recognition that, in a technologically advanced society, most people are powerless to remedy errors or avoid fatal breakdown because of their ignorance. The specialized knowledge required to understand the electrical wiring of a large block of flats — to take only the most simple instance — is not available to most of us. It is made to work for us by those who know; it is not something we are aware of doing or making, not something for which we have any sense of responsibility. So if it should go wrong, producing disaster, pain, death, this is something done *to* us. Uncontrollable force has been unleashed against us, and we are helpless victims.

This is a fairly obvious reading of a fairly obvious fantasy — which of us has not had at least moments of stomach-turning anxiety in an aeroplane, the sense of tempting fate by doing something so complicated as flying? And since September 11, when several nightmares of this kind were realised at once, the anxiety is likely to be more intense. How many commentators remarked that the scenes of that terrible day were 'like a disaster movie'? But there are other nightmares. A close relation to the disaster movie is the fantasy of occult terror, from *The Exorcist* to *The Ring*. Deeper and more irrational dread is involved here: what if the world is populated by powerful, hostile, more-or-less-personal forces that we can't see, hear or touch and have no recognized means of dealing with? They can see us, they are stronger than we, and they work in ways of which we have practically no knowledge. Here again, the violence involved in fantasies of the occult or paranormal is what is done *to* us, it is a force unleashed against us. The power to hurt and destroy is alienated from human possession and transferred to other agencies, and so it becomes uncontrollable. And of course in a secular society, which has no tradition of 'skills' in dealing with, interpreting or resisting the paranormal, it is easy to understand why this is a field in which extreme and neurotic fear has free play.

A major image here is that of the possessed child. The one who is both victim and point of entry for diabolical force is someone who is not an adult and not precisely a full member of society. And this seems to represent a blurring of two different sorts of perception. On the other hand, children (even teenagers) can stand for innocence and vulnerability: as victims of the alien power, they can be images for ourselves, equally innocent, equally vulnerable. Yet they are also the agents of the devil; some writers have pointedly observed that the fantasy of one's children being 'possessed' is one congenial to a generation of parents faced with incomprehensible rebellion from their children. There can be no 'reason' for revolt; and so it is tempting to think of it as imposed upon them. They are being manipulated unawares by invisible enemies of immense resourcefulness and subtlety . . .

That is a theme we shall have to come back to. But it is at this point that the 'paranormal' fantasy begins to shade into the closely related one of insane violence — the psychopathic mass murderer who waits in the back streets of cities, in isolated rural districts, on the edges of the youth camp, and so on. He (the masculine pronoun is deliberate) is again specially interested in the vulnerable and the marginal, and is a particular threat to the lone woman (the number of recent films involving pathological violence against women is striking). In this area, it is not so much a matter of violence done to *us;* there is a much stronger voyeuristic element, especially for the reader or viewer who is not young, female or alone. But the violence still has the same curiously amoral quality, it is done by an agent outside the ordinary range of social control and reasoned decision. The violence of a psychopath is not all that far removed from a natural disaster — or from the 'violence' of an animal.

So this kind of fantasy relates closely to a final category in which the human element is almost entirely removed — imaginings of uncontrollable animal attack, by sharks, wolves, rats, and other natural villains of the animal world. These vary from the fairly naturalistic (like the immortal *Jaws*) to the wildly implausible (the giant ape/prehistoric monster family of fictions). Somewhere in between lie stories of unimaginably huge plagues of beasts or birds, multiplied in number and in strength (even increased in size) by some chance development — perhaps a technological slip, which would neatly combine this with our first category. Science fiction in the narrower sense can reflect the same concerns, and articulate once more the feeling that things are too complex: we have intruded upon areas where we should not go, because we do not know enough to deal with what we might meet. Nature will be revenged on our presumption. That highly imaginative series of space fantasies, *Alien,* manages to combine all this with something rather like the 'possession' theme. There may, then, be a vague sense of culpability in this sort of fiction, yet it is badly focused: guilt about 'interfering with nature' is an ambiguous thing, since no one (quite rightly) is able to say that this is a matter of simple or self-evident good and evil. The 'Faustian' worry — have we gone too far? — is an uneasiness in which it is hard to disentangle real moral concern from the mere dread of increased responsibility.

The family resemblances between all these types of fantasy have to do with the source and nature of violence: all of them clearly reflect the sense that violence is something done *to* us by agencies over which we have no control. It isn't even a question of apportioning 'guilt' for violence to someone else: the agents of it are beyond or below moral assessment. Violence 'happens'. Without real human causes, without roots, without a history, tremendous destructive energies surge up to mutilate and kill. In a sense, they cannot help it any more than we can; psychopaths, animals, natural or supernatural forces simply obey their own inner laws. And the conclusion that is implied in all this is that violence is never something ordinary human beings *decide to do.*

I think this implication is still there in the way these fantasies deal with people's reactions to the unpredictable attacks made on them. There certainly are reactions, countermeasures are taken, and often they are bloody and extreme. Those thought to be 'possessed', for example, can be tied up, beaten, deprived, and so on (which is of course just how such people have so often been treated in our history); animals can be mutilated and killed. It sounds violent enough; but because it is legitimate and unavoidable defence, it will not count as 'real' violence. As a natural and instinctive reaction, it is rather like the attack which provokes it in having very little to do with choice and morality. Extreme circumstances dictate harsh and dramatic responses.

So if we try to feel our way towards a general sense of what the contemporary fantasy world is telling us about violence and destruction, the result seems to be this: pain and injury and sudden death are unpredictable, not planned or chosen by anyone like ourselves, yet always threatening, always around the corner. Against this threat, we defend ourselves as the situation dictates — without many qualms about how we do so, because we are not dealing with agents like ourselves, whose motives and methods would need scrutiny, about whom we might be able to make considered predictions. Violence does not belong in the moral world; it has nothing to do with human responsibility, with the kinds of choices by which we make up our lives from day to day. You could almost say that it is a non-human phenomenon, in the sense that it is so strange and specialized a happening. And it always begins 'somewhere else' — in the mysterious and uncontrollable world Out There.

A society's mass fantasies are anything but trivial, and I do not think we have anything to gain by underrating or simply mocking them. It is all very well to say that nobody with a grain of intelligence 'takes these things seriously'. But what does it mean to 'take them seriously'? Granted that people do not, on the whole, *believe* that they are going to be devoured by plagues of giant rats, possessed by demons as arbitrarily as they might catch a cold, invaded by parasites from outer space, and so on, why are these images so magnetic? Why do even those who, in the cold light of day, would laugh off such things, provide the public for them? There may be nothing very new in some of the themes of such fantasy (H. G. Wells anticipated quite a lot of them), but, if the station bookstall and the cinema are anything to go by, they are now more dominant and compulsive images than they have been. Societies give themselves away in their favourite fantasies; they betray their assumptions about what the world is really like. And that is a very good reason for taking popular fantasy with a great deal of seriousness.

On the basis of what we have looked at so far, it certainly seems as though our society is aware of enormous but badly-defined threats — some internal (arising from the complications of technology), but most external. It is, as a result, tense and afraid, and alarmingly confused because it cannot locate the real sources of danger. More disturbingly, though, it is incapable of seeing this as a *moral* problem — as something to do with power, vision, understanding and choice, with the ways in which we decide to make sense of our lives. And it is incapable of turning a critical eye on itself, asking how far the condition of chronic insecurity it experiences has roots in its own preferences and options. Instead, it chooses to see itself as innocent and vulnerable, recognizing that the world is full of destructive potential, but refusing to deal with this recognition in human moral terms.

It is a kind of fatalism; but as we have noted already, it leaves room for defensive action, which does not in any way diminish our innocence. If we do not and cannot ask about the origins of our experience of a threat of destructive violence, our reactions can only be dictated by that present experience. The situation alone will justify how we act, because analysis and longer perspective are more or less impossible. Long-range calculation about the effects of our 'defensive action' is not the most important thing, because in a fatalistic world it is impossible to see how the situation might escalate.

The picture that emerges is not a very cheering one. It suggests a society very uncomfortable with responsibility. Now we are fairly familiar with the language that opposes rights to responsibilities and complains that we are so in love with the former that we forget the latter; but this is not quite the point at issue here. It is not so much that we are bad at identifying duties as that, corporately, we are not good at seeing our society critically and of acting and planning with some degree of shared awareness. And such a critical perspective would also involve some serious sense of history, a willingness to understand how we got to be what we are and to see that how things are is not natural or eternal but results from decisions made — and not made — and quite a lot of things that are not controllable yet require from us a conscious and intelligent response.

On such a basis, our European/North Atlantic world does not rate very successfully as 'responsible'. From the public language of politicians and a good deal of the media, we might rather glean a picture of pervasive fear and self-pity. We are afraid of our identity being submerged, afraid of government and regulation, afraid of unregulated developments (in the UK, unlimited immigration, for example), afraid of those who will attack and corrupt our children, afraid of terrorism. I do not comment on the rightness or fairness of such fears at this point, only on their pervasiveness, their feverish expression in so much of our public talk. When individuals present symptoms of obsessional fear, we worry about their mental health; perhaps we should worry about our corporate mental health, if such a lot of our public currency has to do with fear. An inability to look truthfully and critically at yourself is a condition of health; for the Christian, it is about the capacity for 'penitence'. To be impenitent is not (or not always) to be bold and hardened in vice, a Byronic villain shouting defiance; it is more often to be afraid of looking at yourself and afraid of changing yourself. 'Impenitence' seems to be a real danger in our context.

But where does the paralysing fear come from? Since the Second World War, the West has lived with a rather bewildering awareness of its own power, economic, military and cultural. It has shaped the agenda of the rest of the world, just by being what it is, so it appears. Yet this power has not delivered much sense of security or ease. Just because it so effectively sets the pace for everyone else, it sets up sharp contrasts, resistances: it generates new kinds of enmity. For the long years of the Cold War, this took the form of an arms race with the Soviet bloc which constantly sought both superiority and stability. Western access to the hydrogen bomb prompted Soviet research to match it; from then on, the pace of competition became increasingly frenzied; even when 'mutual assured destruction' was promised by the balance of terror, there was and could be no absolute stability. Research continued and so the map went on changing. The 'Star Wars' proposal of a nuclear shield, briefly popular in the eighties and revived by the second Bush administration, represented an effort at stabilisation, but with the effect of solidifying the unassailable power of one side. The collapse of Soviet Communism in any case delivered a situation where US military power stood alone on the world stage, with all the highly problematic results that unchallengeability brings with it.

During this era, there was a prevalent state of denial about the nature of the conflict: the Other Side was assumed to be capable of inhuman slaughter on an unparalleled scale; so the preparation of weapons which could effect inhuman slaughter on an unparalleled scale must be justified. The threat of unprecedented violence is an uneasy thing to live with, in both senses — we do not like being threatened with it, but neither do we like threatening to bring it about; there is a strong incentive to insist upon the responsibility of the Other Side for forcing us into such behaviour. We continue to see ourselves as victims, driven to threaten retaliation by the horror of our circumstances. It is not a climate conducive to honesty or to anything like dispassionate analysis of the actual morality of what we are threatening to do.

'Wise people, when they are in the wrong, always put themselves in the right by finding fault with the people against whom they have sinned'; so Trollope claims, in *Barchester Towers*. The rhetoric of the Cold War era had a strong element of this about it, at least to the extent that our own wrongful threat of nuclear destruction could be ascribed to the pressure upon us of the diabolical greed and aggressiveness of the others; it was possible to represent the policies of ceaseless nuclear expansionism as not really 'our' act at all, but something forced on us. Does this do anything to explain the mixed sense of power and helplessness that some of our fantasies reflect? I suspect it may. We are powerful enough to defend ourselves, but that defence is planned in a mode fraught with moral questions; we are not easily allowed to feel good about it, and so must bracket the whole discussion of the ethics of nuclear annihilation with the caveat that of course we should never use our weapons; they are there precisely to prevent the necessity of their own use. This is not complete nonsense, but it has its share of problems as a coherent policy; and it does not make for any degree of real candour about who and where we are. If, in a society shaped by this sort of reasoning, individuals show signs of confusion about responsibility and a strong attraction towards the role of victim, it should not surprise us too much.

The nuclear race in its classic form seems to be more or less over — which is not to say that the nuclear threat is any less serious, given the diffusion of lethal technology from the fragmenting Soviet Union and elsewhere; the discussion over 'weapons of mass destruction' in recent conflicts should have reminded us that this story is not at an end. But in place of the Cold War's drama, we now face the new issue of global terrorism: an enemy hard to locate, not confined to a geographical area, not reliant on large-scale and expensive armaments, recruiting constantly, with a motivation that is disturbingly opaque to us in the North Atlantic world. If anything, this intensifies the tension between power and helplessness; there is no dispute about American military capacity, no rival world power any longer, yet this is a might that cannot achieve its ends or deliver a secure environment, peace and prosperity. Irrational evil seems to lurk undetectably and persistently around every corner and has to be fought at all costs. And anyone raising the question of whether terrorism is best combated by the exercise of large-scale force is promptly accused of appeasing terror or even colluding with it. We must be seen to be making a robust response, otherwise we are letting go of such power as we have, such power as we know how to exercise. Asking how else power could be used is an uncomfortable question, and is quite effectively countered by accusations of disloyalty or cowardice. But the facts on the ground do not allow the questions to be silenced quite so promptly; the aftermath of the Iraq conflict suggests that intensive military intervention in a threatening but non-combatant state can actually — in a highly inflammable regional context — stimulate more terrorist activity.

I had better be clear. I do not believe that terrorism is ever anything but morally outrageous: the deliberate slaughter of the innocent as a deliberate tactic is always wicked. And I do not believe that terrorists are not responsible for their actions: complex operations of mass killing take a lot of planning, and are not simply the work of desperate impoverished victims with no other resort. But: when you have defined terrorism as a strategy of intimidation through indiscriminate killing, you have set up a moral standard by which your own behaviour may be measured. This is not to say that there is 'moral equivalence' between the terrorist and the combatant in the ranks of the Western alliances. This is another cliché of the polemic against those who query the tactics of those alliances. Of course there are different kinds of violence and different degrees of atrocity and of culpability and of legal defensibility.

The cluster bombing of a village in Afghanistan and the suicide bombing of a restaurant in Israel are both acts involving known and to some extent calculated innocent casualties; as such they are both open to moral challenge, especially if the evil of the one becomes part of the justification of the other. *This does not mean that they have to be judged indistinguishable on moral grounds;* a longer argument is required about their respective status. But the reasons for deploring one are at the very least reasons for deploring the other — whether to the same extent or not could not be quickly determined in the abstract. And again: terrorists are people making choices for which they are responsible; but if we are not to conclude that they are totally irrational, motivated only by hatred for certain other races or faiths, we need to ask about what brings them to such a point if we are ever to attempt to change minds or to pre-empt such decisions.

In any case, the situation we now find ourselves in has something in common with the Cold War deadlock. We are being 'backed' into certain sorts of violence against an enemy whose humanity and rationality cannot be taken for granted, with whom the only effective weapon is massive counterforce (which may include erosions of civil liberties or the legal rights of suspects and of prisoners of war). We are reacting; so what we do is not our own freely chosen action. Our morally uneasy policies are forced upon us. Critical self-examination is not readily accessible in this climate. If we are forced into violence, we need all the more desperately to be innocent (and the rhetoric of terrorists themselves shows just this urge to be no more than a driven victim).

At the same time, there is little conviction around that the strategies in use will actually be successful. Just as in the Cold War era surprisingly large numbers of people assumed there would be a major war before the end of the twentieth century, so now there is widespread belief that further terrorist assaults of the utmost gravity are to be expected. It is as if no-one, despite our democratic systems, believes that it is possible for people to make sure that what they most deeply desire politically can actually happen — that they can find a government that will make them safe; and this has been made worse by the widespread sense of a 'democratic deficit' in the processes leading up to the Iraq war. The mentality of some of our modern democracy has, bizarrely, produced a similar mindset to that of totalitarianism — passivity and cynicism. And if we are using popular culture as some kind of barometer of underlying fears, we might notice in passing the success of new fictions based on the premise that the reality we see is in fact 'unreal', manipulated by unseen forces to control us — the most extended and sophisticated such fiction being the *Matrix* series. There have been conspiracy fictions galore in the past; but there is something new in the idea that an entire environment is somehow false, a deliberately illusory construction. And the pervasive feeling that elected government is constantly losing ground to the influence of multinational financial interests fuels this anxiety.

So the picture becomes darker. Not only do we have the 'totalitarian' mentality, the conviction that nothing we do or want is going to make a difference to our fate; we are also convinced that those whose actions determine our fate are no more genuinely free than we are. It is not that we fear that those in power will make a foolish or wicked decision: they

will be victims like us. Victims of what? It is not easy to say —
but people certainly do speculate on the possibility of war being
unleashed by some kind of technical accident (a resurgence of the old nightmare of an over-complex technology), or
they wonder uneasily about the mental health of the powerful.
But it is in any case as if an iron law of ever-growing probability exerted its own compulsion. It will not be chosen, but it
will still happen.

Some readers may be feeling by now that I have made far
too much of the nature of our fantasies, and that it is itself a
fantasy to relate the mentality of *Jaws*, *The Exorcist* or *Alien* to a
society threatened by war and terror. Possibly; but I still believe that we should be putting the question of why this particular kind of disaster-fantasy is so prevalent among us. Whatever the exact explanation, it unmistakably reflects fear and
powerlessness at once; and few would want to deny that a major incentive for feelings of fear and powerlessness is the menace of unqualified and irrational violence. What our collective
nightmares do for us is not to remove a fear that is perfectly
well-grounded, but to reinforce our unwillingness to think
about these matters in terms of guilt and responsibility. That is
why I decided to begin these reflections by looking at our fantasy life. If these dreams are fulfilling a function for us — and
dreams do perform necessary jobs for us in helping us to live
with our tensions and conflicts — and that function is chiefly
one of confirming our innocence, it is right to be suspicious
about what it is in our world that makes it so urgent to avoid
the feeling of guilt.

We are intensely aware of danger, of the real and potential
violence in our environment; and we are deeply determined to

imagine violence as something whose origins lie outside ourselves, so that we can maintain some belief in our innocence. But the price of this is a real uneasiness and confusion about what we can and cannot do, about the nature of our power and freedom. For all the talk about this freedom, or indeed of the 'free world', we seem to be taking it for granted in several ways that we are not free at all: our decisions are constrained by the violence of others, and our governments cannot be relied on to deliver what we really want. And to feel removed from effective decision-making in such ways is risky for any population: it breeds the politics of do-it-yourself extremism (the far right, trading always on the perception that government has subverted a nation's 'real' identity), which flourishes still more when the rest of the population feels alienated from the whole process. The greatest danger is when extremism begins to set the pace and decisions at a high level are moulded by this sort of pressure; democratic governments can end up carrying through policies that in the cold light of day a population would not and could not morally endorse; and the schism at the heart of modern politics becomes worse and worse.

Christian theology tries consistently to keep us focused on two apparently contradictory truths. We are radically dependent — limited, subject to change and chance, not fully in charge of our circumstances; and we are free and responsible for our human, political and physical environment. In the face of denials of guilt and fantasies of innocence, the gospel tells us that we have to repent, to take responsibility for what we have made of our world and beg for vision and strength to do better. In the face of apathy and fatalism, the gospel requires us to ask where differences can be made and what precisely our part might be in realising this. In the face of obsessions about security and control, the gospel reminds us that we are made who we are in dependence on each other and on our creator. The gospel provides the energy of truthfulness and the ability to go beyond fear. It not only asks for repentance, it makes it possible, and gives us the skills to discern where we do and do not have power, refusing to allow us to settle for either the myth of being innocent victims who never really *do* anything or the myth of omnicompetence, in which there are no insoluble problems for human beings.

Of course it is a mistake, and a serious one, to overestimate the power we have to change things in even the most resolutely democratic institutions. But the disowning of responsibility is undoubtedly the mark of a deep sickness of the spirit, struggling to keep pain, horror and destruction away from the sphere of my soul, my desires and hopes. And this sickness, while it appears to be a way of protecting ourselves, in fact prevents us from using our spiritual resources to confront and assimilate the pain and guilt we cannot bear.

A psychotherapist,[1] writing on 'the Bomb as an instrument of mass suicide', has said that the process of 'deadening of feelings and fragmentation of the mind', of neurotic and hopeless flight from reality, is prompted partly by the pace and the scale of catastrophe in this century. We have already — in the World Wars, in the Holocaust, in famine and genocide, and, less drastically, in the destruction of families and environments — seen more devastation than we can easily cope with. We are losing the capacity to 'mourn' — to draw on reserves of compassion

1. Dr. Nini E. Ettlinger.

that help us to re-affirm values, feeling the enormity of pain and death and violence, and feeling it because we have a richer and better hope for men and women. When there is no time or energy to mourn because there is too much to mourn for, hopelessness takes over, accompanied by the lack of a sense of responsibility. And so, faced with the risk of nuclear annihilation and terrorist slaughter on top of all the other horrors of the last seventy years, it is understandable that such a sickness should prevail.

It is a way of buying a certain kind of 'peace'. It does not do away with fear, but it does at least seem to ease the moral strain. It absolves us from facing the humiliating picture of ourselves as idle, self-indulgent and culpably ignorant, suggested when we take our freedom seriously. We do not have to think about guilt. Yet — as we have already remarked — this means that repentance is not a possibility; and if repentance is impossible, so is grace, reconciliation, hope. So this is a 'peace' which must be unmasked for the lie it is — peace bought at the cost of reality, at the cost of human dignity. Our evasive fantasies must be brought to judgement before we can be brought to grace.

In our day more than ever, war and peace are 'spiritual' as well as tactical and political issues. We shall not understand our society and its terrors and anxieties about total war unless we grasp that behind these anxieties lies a profound sickness of spirit; and it is a sickness which only succeeds in reinforcing the structures that give rise to it in the first place.

Gospel, good news, for a society like ours must involve a clear and accurate diagnosis of this kind of sickness, because only so will it become possible to open the doors of repentance once again. Just as in individual therapy it is so important to restore to people the power to mourn, to reawaken both sensitivity and hope, so for society at large war — or rather warlikeness — produces the crippled spirits of totalitarianism. War is to be dreaded (if we can echo the words of Jesus) not so much because it kills the body as because it destroys both body and soul, because its casualties are health and truth and hope. To resist this destruction is to affirm a faith in a human future; and the Gospel, by driving us to penitence, grounds this affirmation of the future in the loving will of God, remaking us through our conversion.

To be 'converted' means, in this connection, to retrieve the vision of one's own responsibility, and to learn to look in critical openness at one's own life and the shared life of society around. So that conversion is also vocation — the call to *be* free, to take up responsibility and work out how it can be exercised, even in the most apparently unpromising circumstances. We can, of course, make the mistake of thinking that the Gospel prescribes simple answers to the problem of working this out — so that some solutions, which seem obvious to us, are given the authority of the Gospel itself. But the world we live in is a world in which we do not have clear paths open before us; we are not able normally to decide on a simple course of action and carry it through without opposition or the need for adjustment and adaptation. There is a huge difference between recovering a sense of the power to choose and to act in hope, and acquiring a sense of power *over* things, power to shape the world as I want it. And to learn to live with the truth that the latter is an empty illusion is a great part of what we mean by moral maturity.

The Gospel frees us from fear and fantasy, from the nightmares of guilt and insecurity which paralyse our imagination and so prevent us from positive and meaningful action. But precisely because it is the great enemy of self-indulgent fantasy, it frees us into a real world where flexibility and discrimination are vital. I have avoided using the word 'compromise' for this — partly for the simple reason that it is a 'negative' word in most people's minds, and partly because I suspect that there *is* a distinction between a mere readiness to come to a workable arrangement and a sensitivity to the many, often unsatisfactory, means needed to attain a vision or a goal.

I have spoken about discernment. It is what makes Christian theology cautious about absolutely clear and would-be final analyses and prescriptions in this complex area of peacemaking. Classical pacifism has not always provided anything like a mature analysis of power and of how power can be used non-violently; it has been weak on the details of active peacemaking and conciliation. But it should be impossible for a Christian to settle comfortably with existing assumptions about the management of conflict in our world. This chapter has attempted to suggest ways of identifying some of the imaginative and moral cost of the denial and displacement that has been so prevalent in our attitudes to international and intercultural conflicts in the last few decades. We still live with a 'default position' in which an innocent party is forced into threat, violence or repression by a wilfully guilty one. Without going for the equally facile and delusive picture of equal evil and corruption all round ('we are all guilty'), our corporate health requires both an awareness of this seductive mechanism for preserving an innocent image and a willingness to think around the problem to avoid being trapped in a constantly repeating cycle of aggression and reprisal.

The Christian community might well be accused, in the biblical phrase, of 'healing the wound of my people lightly, saying "Peace, peace", when there is no peace' (Jeremiah 6.14), if it failed to insist on these requirements for corporate health in our society. The wound needs exposing; when the late Dennis Potter spoke of religion as 'the wound, not the bandage' in the memorable interview he gave during his last illness, he may have been thinking of the ways in which faith has to expose unwelcome truths because faith has the resource to confront them without despair. But how does the Church itself become a peaceful community? Its own inner life is regularly the site of bitter and destructive conflict, and its interventions in the public square, especially on matters of war and peace and international affairs are readily characterised (and written off) as both abstract and amateur. Often they are; but it remains true that the rationale of the Church's life is irreducibly a matter of showing the results of an act of divine reconciliation in terms of a distinctive kind of human community. What are the distinguishing marks? And how can they be set to work? In what follows, I do not attempt a programme for the churches, but I do attempt to clarify a few things about these distinguishing marks which belong to the sheer existence of the Church, however disappointingly the Church manages in making them real and useful. If the bare existence of the Church is a challenge, as it should be, to passivity, fatalism, false innocence and false claims to power, it is worth spending some time exploring why this is. And it is worth hoping that out of this will emerge, not a programme to resolve all conflict, but at least a sense of what is asked of believers that is different from the prevailing accounts of peace, conflict, guilt and human possibility.

2 The Truce of God

In the early Middle Ages, the great Burgundian monastery of Cluny sponsored and encouraged an experiment in conciliation among its feudal neighbours — half-civilized landlords in a state of more or less endemic war with each other. The arrangement, known as 'the truce of God', was that all hostilities should be restricted to three days in the week (Monday to Wednesday). Of course, this was never observed for any length of time with much consistency; and in retrospect its mixture of naïve earnestness and cynicism is rather funny (very characteristic of the Church, somehow . . .). But it is more than a comical bit of mediaeval eccentricity. Behind it lay the recognition that for baptized Christians, sharers in the Body of Christ, to be in a state of war with one another was horrible and ridiculous. The mild ludicrousness of the response pales, however, in comparison with the absurdity of people, who could in principle kneel side by side to share the communion of Christ's body and blood, also planning revengeful slaughter against each other.

Mediaeval Christians seem very odd to most of us today, and nothing is helped by romanticizing them in a G. K.

Chesterton style. But there are points at which they really do challenge us very sharply. They had a certain instinctive sense that symbols were not a matter simply of decoration, but both declared and actualized certain policies for meaningful living. Thus there were, for them, situations in which they could not treat actions as 'just' symbolic. When King Henry II refused to give the kiss of peace at Mass to Thomas Becket, he was a better theologian than he knew. He recognized that giving the kiss would not only suggest that he *was* at peace with Thomas (which he was not) but would also commit him to *seeking* peace (which he did not want to do). He knew well enough that he had no intention of giving the symbol room to work; and so, rightly and honestly, he sinned boldly and refused it.

During the Cold War years, a number of theologians — including the great Karl Barth — argued passionately that the nuclear standoff implied a situation in which members of Christ's Church had made themselves unable to perform such symbolic acts with honesty. If it was true (as manifestly it was) that the Church did not stop at the physical or cultural boundaries of 'the West', what was involved in systematically threatening mass destruction against those on the wrong side of those boundaries? We should hardly say — should we? — that we'd have to refuse to exchange the kiss of peace with a visiting Christian from the old Soviet Union or East Germany; but perhaps it would have been more candid to do so.

But the point can be extended beyond the terms simply of what is owed to members of the Body of Christ. The Church exists to be in itself a symbol of God's purpose for a reconciled humanity; as such it works on the assumption that we do not yet know where the boundaries of the Body of Christ might finally lie. It cannot assume that this or that group is ultimately unreconcilable to God or to the rest of humanity. This is not because of any sentimental preconceptions about the natural goodness of human beings, but because of a conviction that the call of God can be addressed to any human person or community, and that it is the same call to compassion, justice, conscious and responsible love. Thus policies which involve wholesale slaughter or which rest on indiscriminate demonisation of a real or potential enemy cannot be squared with the kind of thing the Church is. Just by being itself, the Church will put a question to any such distorted ideas. The Church proclaims that there is one human destiny and that it is found in relation to one focal figure, Jesus; but also that what this human destiny means cannot be worked out without 'communion', a relation of profound and costly involvement with each other and receiving from each other. This and this alone is what saves the proclamation of Christ's uniqueness from being a piece of ideological tyranny. Only as each different 'other' becomes a friend and a member of the Body can we discern how the unity of the Body will look; we do not begin with a blueprint which is to be forced on the stranger, or even a timetable and a programme for how they must accept the gospel. It is a matter of looking at the stranger with candour, patience and hope, in the trust that our common destiny can be uncovered by the grace of Christ.

This is what the Church exists to say, and to sing, play, paint, act in all the ways it can: that human destiny, for all its unpredictable and irreducible differences, is in fact a single pattern organized around the magnetic centre of Jesus. And this means that my human vocation is part of the same harmonic whole as yours. To affirm my calling is to affirm yours in the same moment. If Jesus's humanity, Jesus's way of living and dying, is the shape of my future, so it is for all; no section, no class or nation within the human world, is excluded in advance from the hope of this calling. And thus there is not one Christian hope for one group, another for the rest — a point perhaps worth making against over-exclusive styles of black theology or women's theology or even liberation theology. In the long run, liberation is indivisible for those who truly believe that the world holds together in the one Word which is Jesus.

The Church, then, is a sign both of God's comprehensive, unified purpose and of its embodiment in Jesus; but also of the humanity that is to be — a global family, in which God's gifts are thankfully received *to be shared,* and all are involved in building up the liberty and maturity of all. The Church is a place where we are invited to look at one another with a kind of veneration, indeed, a kind of contemplation, delighting in the rich possibilities which our brothers and sisters have — and weeping over all those things which distort or block those possibilities. 'Who is weak, and I am not weak?' asked St. Paul (2 Corinthians 11:29): the frustration or oppression of anyone is a diminution of my own strength and my own possibilities (which is why so many see certain attitudes to the ordained ministry of women in the Church as a weakening or a diminution of all ministry). So while the Church does not exist for the sake of peace, it is not easy to see how the Church can truly be itself in the absence of peace, in a situation where — by definition — people see the interests of various groups or nations as mutually exclusive.

But of course, because of the infinite possibilities of self-deceit in human beings, there will always be some such absence of peace. False and blasphemous goals are fixed, false models of humanity prevail. And in such circumstances there will be conflict, and rightly so — conflict sometimes between the Church and the society in which it lives, because that society is in bondage to idols. Indeed, much of the point of what I wrote in the first chapter was to suggest that we need to identify more clearly certain points of sharp collision or contradiction between the Christian vision and the prevailing mind of our society. In this sense, the Church is never going to be completely itself while history lasts — or, in more traditional theological terms, the Church and the world will never completely coincide. We live in hope, and to the extent we live in hope, we also live in creative dissatisfaction.

However, the Church does exist — not perfectly, but still quite concretely. Within its own life it is found to be a sacrament, an effective, compelling symbol, of a humanity able to live by sharing and by loving, reverent mutual attention. In its life it is committed to challenging the conventional conflicts of power and interest in the world. We all know how effectively a multi-racial Church can operate as a point of hope and criticism in a racially divided society. And any situation where we allow ourselves to settle for a view implying that our good and our survival are necessarily secured by treating the other as dispensable will be unsustainable for the Christian believer.

The existence of the Church announces that we all need each other for our fulfilment, and that when mutual sharing breaks down this is a universal tragedy, a wound in the whole human race. The logical conclusion is indeed what a great Russian saint of this century said, that no one could truly know the joys of heaven so long as anyone remained in hell. And the same insight lies behind one of the central beliefs of certain Buddhists: no enlightened person, no 'Buddha', can enter into ultimate bliss while there are still unenlightened souls on earth. The greater the enlightenment, the greater the compassion; so the enlightened saint returns again and again to earth (like the Dalai Lama) for the sake of the ignorant and suffering.

If salvation is for any, it is for all. And Christianity in its way goes even further than Buddhism by coming near to suggesting that if it is not for all, it is not really for any. The 'return' to the lost, the excluded, the failed or destroyed, is not an option for the saint, but the very heart of saintliness. And we might think not only of Jesus's parable of the shepherd, but of the great theological myth of the Descent into Hell, in which God's presence in the world in Jesus is seen as his journey into the furthest deserts of despair and alienation. It is the supreme image of his freedom, to go where he is denied and forgotten; he shows his inexhaustible mercy for all by identifying even with the lost. In some elusive and paradoxical way, this myth speaks yet again of one human destiny, realized in and through Jesus. He comes to his new and risen life, his universal kingship, by searching out *all* the forgotten and failed members of the human family. Only in this way can he claim 'all authority in heaven and on earth'; only in this way can his family be in principle co-extensive with the whole human family, past, present and to come.

Our hope and our faith as Christians is that Jesus is Lord —

that there is no situation in which he is irrelevant or impotent. In all human experience, even the most hellish, he is present, his image can be found, as a point of creative protest, growth and change. And this we believe because he endured the extreme of lostness himself on his path to the throne of his Father; he enters into his glory in and through the enduring of our human hell. In other words, our faith absolutely depends on an unimaginable crossing of frontiers, the barriers between God and despairing, Godless men and women. It depends on the possibility of meeting Christ in any and every place, and in any and every person. The degree to which we fail to find him, see or hear him, in anyone, is the degree to which we have not grasped — or rather yielded to, been grasped by — his Lordship.

And that is why the Church is 'catholic' — for all, adapting itself endlessly to human culture and to human need, opening itself to all, and linking the cultures and needs, the various identities, the diverse roots, of men and women the world over. It strives to show and interpret and share the gifts of one person or group or nation, offering them to all; and to each it offers the resources of all. When it is not catholic, it is not truly itself (hence the seriousness of the division between Christian communions — the deeper the split, the less freely grace works in the divided groups, because they are refusing the unique gifts they should be receiving through each other). And when it is, however sporadically and unsurely, catholic, it is a sacrament of peace: not a peace of undramatic, tepid co-existence and noninterference, but a peace which is free, active involvement, compassion, grateful receiving, generous offering, reciprocal enrichment. This is the peace Jesus creates between God and world, because it is the kind of peace which exists between him and his Father. We shall be looking at this later in more detail; perhaps for now we can let it stand as a general and provisional definition at the most basic theological level of what the Church is about in relation to the life and death of Jesus.

So, returning to our starting-point: a catholic Church is one whose loyalty is to a vision of humanity as a single, though endlessly various, whole, a single pattern centred on Jesus. Its loyalties cannot be nationalistic or even ideological. Its very existence on both sides of an international ideological conflict challenges the all-importance or finality of that conflict. This does not mean that such conflicts are of no concern to Christians, or that Christianity is 'beyond' conflict. It *does* mean that any attitude which implies that the survival of my/our point of view/national security/purity of doctrine is so absolute a priority that no human price in the lives or welfare of others is too high to pay for it, is intolerable for the Christian.

Of course, people in positions of public responsibility constantly make judgements in which a price is paid in the welfare and the life of some: there is 'moral risk' involved here, and there is no point in minimizing its seriousness. Those concerned for peace too easily ignore its cost. Yet there is surely an irreconcilable collision; the Church really does relativize our loyalties, denying totally that the survival or success of one human sector or interest can ever be a final priority such as to justify the destruction of the dissidents. There are situations where violent resistance seems to many the only available option, as was the case in the struggle with Nazism — or indeed the local military intervention that overthrew Idi Amin. It was an argument much in evidence in discussion about the regime of Saddam Hussein. It will not do for Christians just to condemn and distance themselves from such argument. But the force of the argument does not resolve all moral difficulties at a stroke: the question of what makes intervention *lawful* is a long and complex one, one in which considerations of prudence and ordinary political virtue and the difference between acceptable and impossible moral cost to an intervening power all play a substantial part. What ought not to be on the agenda is any possibility for the Church to rejoice in a decision for armed conflict or to deny its cost.

And so the catholic Church must be a standing challenge to all war-oriented policy; above all to a policy which deliberately and regularly speaks in terms of retaliation and a balance of terror. How could such rhetoric be justified, except on the assumption that our interests are a priority for which no price is too high — the very assumption which the catholic Gospel utterly contradicts? No Christian can use this kind of language without a profound betrayal of faith in the lordship of Jesus crucified, Jesus in hell, Jesus who fills heaven and earth with his compassionate identification, his breaking of barriers. The world is such that we cannot ignore questions of defence and security — only a moral imbecile could fail to see that; yet the concept of a *total* defence purchased by *total* threat, defence through the menace of mutual genocide, takes us beyond morality and reason as much as it takes us beyond faith and charity.

It undermines faith; and it equally undermines penitence. We saw in the first chapter how the social effects of planning for total war work against the possibility of responsible awareness and creative change by generating fantasies of impotence in the face of utterly irrational disaster. But here we are dealing with another kind of alibi for repentance. Repentance, for Christians, is intimately bound up with the hope of change — more particularly, of changed relationships. It is an acknowledgement of failure, based on trust in grace — which is the trust that no breakdown or severance of understanding and contact is ultimately disastrous. We are not forever 'frozen' in the attitudes of greed, envy, malice, manipulation and distrust which ruin so much of our lives. We are not fixed eternally in the distorted relation of oppressor and victim, rejecter and rejected. Repentance is our refusal to close our ears and hearts to the other, our confession that we cannot live without them. And although there are all sorts of situations in which we have no tangible guarantees that reconciliation with another person is achieved or realized, at least we have turned to them with our hands open. Our repentance, our turning around, has introduced something fresh, or rather, has recognized the possibility of grace, the hidden image of Jesus, which is already there in the situation, and allowed it room to emerge.

Planning wholesale destruction is planning impenitence. It represents a choice to fix or freeze relations in the state of total mutual rejection. When you have obliterated the other, in full consciousness of what you are doing, in order precisely to avoid any radical questioning of your own interest, your own secure identity, it is hard to see how penitence could be generated. Perhaps it could; but after a nuclear conflict, it would (if it was going to be at all sincere) be massively traumatic and disorienting. There are those who have repented of their share in the Holocaust; far more seem to know that acknowledgement of what they have done would simply strain their sanity to the breaking-point, and a merciful (though far from grace-ful) amnesia conquers (something I have tried to reflect on in an earlier piece of writing, on resurrection and forgiveness). And it is surely a question worth asking whether any society as a whole could sanely live with such a memory. Would not the result more probably be an intensification of just that desperate flight from responsibility we were looking at in the first chapter?

We need to pause for a moment to consider one of the more complicated aspects of our recent international history. During the most intense years of the arms race in the Cold War years, it was often claimed that the nuclear competition had guaranteed decades of relative peace; a substantial period had passed without a major global war. The collapse of the Soviet bloc was in many people's eyes a vindication of the policy of those years. A balance of power was maintained by repeated upward adjustments of military capacity, until one party became incapable of further adjustment and retired from the contest, leaving one superpower in position, and therefore minimising the risk of global conflict.

The detailed justification of any such analysis will have to wait for the professional historians of the next generation, I suspect. But it is not a claim that can be lightly dismissed. All I want to do is suggest some problems that a Christian might want to raise here. We did indeed experience several decades without a global war; we also saw the development of a pattern of small-scale but often very bloody conflict away from the old European theatres of war and the North American continent. This ranged from Vietnam to Angola to various Latin American states to the Iran-Iraq war and the steadily worsening conflicts in the Holy Land. Some of this was unmistakably a 'displacement' of superpower conflict, a struggle for influence, especially in Africa and the Middle East. Various nations or groups became local surrogates for the United States or the Soviet Union. Even where such conflict was not the original motor of a conflict, the development of the struggle drew in patterns of alliances (and of arms trading) that produced a clearly discernible alignment, as in the Iran-Iraq case: Iran's hostility to the USA (because of US support of an earlier corrupt and oppressive administration) guaranteed that Iran's enemy was judged deserving of US military investment.

In the present climate, there is no longer one obvious story of international struggle into which all local issues must be squeezed (although a moral map of the world in which pro- and anti-Americanism have become the terms of a new grand narrative is clearly visible in the rhetoric of some). But the legacy of these years of displacement is not to be ignored. Patterns of economic dependence have built up, as have patterns of hostility to foreign military manipulation; the arms trade has entered a dizzying spiral of expansion, now much complicated by the availability of nuclear technology to poorer nations; the resentful awareness of being used for the agenda of others has festered, especially in the Islamic world. In other words, the price of peace in the 'developed' world as guaranteed by the nuclear balance was already, twenty years ago, a substantial body count in the 'developing' world; and the longer term cost is visible in the depoliticised, militarised societies that flourish in economically disadvantaged countries, not to mention the emergence of Islamic extremism in ways that Muslim societies (and others) could never remotely have predicted in the sixties and seventies. It is as if the Cold War period was, for many states, particularly in Africa and West Asia, a moratorium in the history of their political modernisation — or worse than a moratorium, a moulding into patterns of dependence or corruption or militarisation. The added role of international debt during this period in reinforcing such patterns would need another book to itself.

Hence my reasons for some scepticism about the peaceful effects of the Cold War era. Honesty requires that we look rather hard at the present realities of Africa and Asia and ask how much responsibility for their condition lies with a mindset in which military and strategic decisions distracted the great powers from coherent development policies and pressed many nations into an artificial mould within the international drama. This is not quite the same as saying that the poverty of developing nations is the result of the wealth of rich ones; economists who deride this as a crude zero-sum version of a far more complex reality are doubtless to a large extent right. But a history of displaced conflict, aggravated by debt, is certainly something to do with the responsibilities of wealthier nations in recent decades; and it is not too much of an exaggeration to say that peace in Europe and North America has been purchased at the cost of systematic destabilisation elsewhere. The current trends towards the export of this instability in the form of pervasive terrorist activity have begun to bring this home to the developed nations. Terrorism is morally appalling, and is itself a symptom of 'depoliticised' thinking (despair of democratic processes, threat as the fundamental language of power, total rejection of the stranger, contempt for negotiation); but the firm acknowledgement of these points should not provide an alibi for looking at what the global context is in which such an option has emerged.

The whole of this chapter has attempted to press the point that the very existence of the Church is a challenge to that view of the world which claims that the welfare of some may rightly be secured by the dispensability of others. In the light of this challenge, the history of the Cold War years and what has followed does not read straightforwardly as a record of the sort of peacekeeping that a Christian can be content with. It will be said that there would have been worse options; indisputably. But we are not called on to assess abstract possibilities but the specific costs of our policies; and the purpose of this is not either to demonstrate their justifiable inevitability or to wring hands over the cost, but to acknowledge the truth and ask how we move on from here in making up the deficit of several decades — in terms of demilitarisation, controls on arms trading, the development of civil society and the fostering of investment in local economies and manageable credit practices.

It is really no more than the imperative to pay attention to those who have carried such a lot of the cost of our 'peace'. Claims about the strategic success of the Cold War years suggest a lack of such attention. For the Christian, the whole story seems an affront to the singleness of Christian hope for the human family, the indivisibility of a future given coherence by Jesus, in which each human partner in communion has a distinct and unrepeatable gift to share, and cannot therefore be ignored or discounted. What if the greatest of our sins in the modern age turned out to be the failure to *look* at other human beings? All the greater for being committed in a context where the means of looking at each other are more developed than ever, through our information systems.

The failure to look, or, to revert to a word used earlier in this connection, the failure to contemplate. Contemplation is what is due to God; due to him because he is inexhaustibly what he is, resisting capture and analysis, always more, always further. But he has not left himself without witnesses, because the world is full of phenomena which, although they may be analysable on one level, resist any kind of total assimilation and continue to invite and question. Art at its best does this. In fact, anything which invites us to the pervasive awareness of a world beyond the power of the ego invites contemplation; which is also why contemplation is inseparable from delight and love, which arise in their full reality, life, and growth only when we are taken out of the sterile closed circle of ourselves and our plans, projects and expectations. 'It was not possible for man to know himself and the world, except first after some mode of knowledge, some art of discovery. The most perfect . . . art was pure love. The approach by love was the approach to fact; to love anything but fact was not love.' Thus Charles Williams, in his most successful treatment of the triumph of illusion and self-gratification in human relations, the novel *Descent Into Hell*. No love without contemplation, no contemplation without a mind and heart open to receive and not seeking to create its own world out of the nothingness of the ego and its fantasies.

Contemplation for men and women is looking and listening and being moulded by what is other. It is recognizing that you are created — limited, living in time — and allowing yourself to go on being created in and by the world of things and persons in time, all of them mediating the obscure universal initiative of an uncreated action, so wholly regardless of 'self' that it lets the whole universe be. Creation is there because of the limitless capacity of *God* for contemplation — allowing the other to be, and engaging with the other, shaping a common story of God and the world, a shared 'drama'. God allows himself to appear in the form of limitation, as if he needed us for his delight and fulfilment — Christ calling for his bride to come out to him and perfect his joy. It is on this that St. John meditates in the 'Farewell Discourses' in his gospel.

God contemplates the world out of his own freedom; it is both his freedom and his nature that he acts to involve himself in covenant and in family relationship with us. It is because of the inexhaustibility of his love that he can show himself in and through limited and mortal beings, in creatures. But we, who are creatures by nature, begin with limited freedom and limited love; so that for us contemplation is something we have to choose and learn and grow into. For God, it is saying Yes to all creation; for us it is saying Yes to our *createdness,* and through that, saying Yes to the createdness of all other things. God in a sense does not 'need' to love and to contemplate a creation: he is in himself attentive love at its highest (which is part of what the doctrine of the Trinity affirms). He loves, speaks, communicates, delights and shares because it is his nature. But what for him is nature is for us destiny, vocation. We are in time, and thus what we are we must grow into. We *do* need contemplation, we need to learn selfless love, because for us there is always the possibility of failing to grow as we should. So we need to live in a world constantly inviting us to contemplation, a world which will not leave us alone, feeding only on ourselves — a world which delights us and which assaults us by its strangeness, its resistance to us. And, above all, a world of persons, in which we can be invited to love by finding ourselves the objects of love, where we learn contemplative attention as we are ourselves attended to.

I hope this will help to make it rather clearer why a system which denies or threatens the contemplative possibilities of human beings is a revolt against the creating will of God. We speak about certain outcomes in national or international affairs as potentially 'apocalyptic' conflicts; the term has become almost too glib, as if talking about the end of the world rolled off the tongue a good deal more readily than it should. And there are not lacking those who say there is a certain lack of faith in undue fear of the end of the world-as-we-know-it, since God's providence is always capable of working through and beyond disaster. True, of course. But it quite ignores the fact, laboured enough already in these pages, that war is not a natural disaster. It occurs because of human greed, fantasy and destructiveness — that is, because of sin. Sin is fundamentally a refusal to accept creatureliness, the struggle to remake the world around myself; it is a refusal of contemplation. To refuse contemplation is to refuse God's creation, and so to reject love. And if hell means anything, it means this. It is this we fear, and rightly fear. Not 'the end of the world' as a catastrophe at the material level (as if that were not bad enough), but the *unmaking* of the world, the system of created relationships designed for sacrificial love — a massive and ultimate revolt against the will of God. Let me reiterate what I wrote earlier: war is to be dreaded because it destroys both body and soul, because, in our present circumstances, it points to hell.

Professor Donald MacKinnon, in his 1981 Boutwood Lectures on 'Ethical Problems of Nuclear Warfare', spoke of the nuclear state as confronted by unprecedented temptation — the temptation to try for 'total victory', 'to yield to a fundamental impatience, the end either total victory or nothingness'. And this is most suggestively linked with Milton's presentation in *Paradise Regained* of the culminating temptation of Jesus by Satan, to cast himself from the pinnacle of the Temple. 'Milton saw Christ tempted impatiently to escape the burden of his human existence. We live in an age in which such a temptation is not far from every one of us; for we have to learn anew what it is to be human.'

What it is to be human: to be a creature, a part of the world, a moment in a pattern, dependent on others, others dependent on ourselves, called therefore to contemplation, without which there is no growth or fullness. Isolation is the refusal of humanity; and that includes the isolation of my or our needs from those of the human world. Beyond it stands the Luciferian impulse to destroy reality for my sake, the impatience with the weary burden of creatureliness. Creatureliness means, after all, never having 'done with' people or the world around or God. It means the risk of response, decision, listening and answering, *attending* to a constantly shifting environment. But to reject all this, hugging to oneself the diabolical knowledge that it could all be ended if we so chose, is the beginning of hell — like Marcus Aurelius' chilling remark that you may console yourself in misery with the reflection that you are always perfectly free to escape from life, though it might be improper actually to do so. Our liberty is thus seen as freedom to cut our ties, to unravel the knots binding us in one world, to break the humiliating cords of interdependence; liberty to be unreal, to commit moral — if not physical — suicide.

God's liberty is not so. His freedom is seen in the creation of bonds and networks of sharing, making a world which he wills, in Jesus and his Church, to be engaged. If we seek God-like liberty, it can only be through the acceptance of that same world — with all the risk involved, the uncertainty. We must say No to the temptation to diabolic detachment, the privacy of Satan; and we must learn the patience of attentive love. Through that vulnerability true peace is made, in us and for us.

Yet, of course, it is an elusive thing. 'Peace' can be the ultimate consoling fantasy, and we need all our alertness to see that it does not become so. Before going on to explore something of what is positively involved in peace-making, we must have a critical look also at some of our illusory images of peace. To this we shall turn in the next chapter.

3 *Illusions of Peace*

P eople go to stay in the guest-houses of monasteries and convents (in surprisingly large numbers) to absorb an atmosphere of 'peace': it is a break from conflict and tension, a move into another world from which strain is supposedly absent. The world of the cloister is one in which some new level of awareness has been attained, and its inhabitants breathe a different air. And we, less fortunate (or less committed), are briefly admitted into it, for our nourishment and refreshment.

We all, in fact, badly need images of achieved repose, of a state in which the process of 'becoming' is in effect over; and we are increasingly fascinated by the contrast between 'being' and 'doing', and more and more inclined to think that a great deal of our civilization has been badly wrong about the balance between the two, overstressing acting, making, imposing change. It is true, too, that a lot of the central images of Christianity are not reposeful: however much the cross of Jesus is softened and formalized, however much the naked figure is clothed as priest or king, it remains an image that speaks of incompleteness, of a world of unreconciled conflicts, because it is inescapably the image of a man being tortured to death. We need something for daily consumption that is a bit less 'unfinished', and so, understandably, we turn to images of the sacred that are more still, more rounded or balanced. Certainly the popularity of the image of Mary has something to do with this — the innocence of virginity and the 'finished achievement' of motherhood hauntingly combined in a symbol of purity which also manages, uniquely, to be a symbol of nurture and inclusion, not simply of remoteness.

And the holiness of the cloister can be a corporate symbol of peace achieved — a thought superbly expressed in Hopkins' little poem, 'Heaven-Haven: A nun takes the veil':

And I have asked to be
Where no storms come,
Where the green swell is in the havens dumb,
And out of the swing of the sea.

This means that Christians living a monastic life have laid upon them an enormous load of expectation. They are called (not by God but by the Church) to make their lives, individually and communally, images of 'peace'. And thus people often feel very deeply hurt and betrayed when such images are broken; when someone leaves a community, re-enters 'our' world, as if to say that there is no decisive release from struggle, that the wheel can still turn. The world of the cloister is not so 'finished' after all, not invulnerable to strain, frustration, unhappiness and the heavy responsibility of choice. Of course we go on as usual with our fictionalized cloisters, full of people with no history, no record of change: the second-rate novel or film blithely continues to present us with the calm, bland stereotype of monk or nun (especially the latter), dedicated but basically untormented. But the closer we are to the reality of the lives of those of our fellow Christians living the religious life, the emptier this fiction becomes, and the clearer it is that the consoling peacefulness we demand to see embodied in them is not there for the asking. We do a serious injustice to the cloister when we dictate its terms of reference to it. Nor is it any excuse that there is also a monastic rhetoric which goes along with the world's fantasies: however lovely and seductive this is (as in Hopkins' poem), it is essentially untruthful; and no one knew that better than Hopkins himself in his own religious life.

Those upset or dissatisfied by Christianity's reluctance to provide adequate images of repose and fulfilment will be liable to look elsewhere. Much of the attraction of Buddhism for the liberal Western mind surely lies in this area: here is a style of action and response (not exactly a 'faith') in which the focal picture is indeed one of repose and disengagement — 'peace' in the sense we desire. The Buddha in meditation, eyes turned inward, so to speak, appears to the Western observer as a symbol of the achieved state in which conflict disappears; it can even, in its simple solidity, look like a figure without tension or the need for balance. Some writers, Eastern and Western, have indeed compared this favourably with the tortured image of the cross, and have made the valid and searching point that the cross itself can become a tool for an unhealthy and destructive obsession with pain. Yet the outside observer of the Buddhist world is all too liable to forget that even this image of repose and transcendence of conflict belongs in a far wider context of story and symbolism and ethical doctrine: balance, flexible imagination ('skill in means'), even conflict all have their role in the Buddhist spectrum. The Buddha's repose is indeed a state 'outside history'. But it represents a balance continually sought and renewed in historical life, and one which (at least for a very large section of the Buddhist world) is expressed in active compassion, a voluntary return into the world of suffering for the sake of those still imprisoned and unenlightened. The ultimate rest of nirvana is an idea, a myth, constantly interacting with the dynamic structures of worldly life, not a state of peacefulness objectively existing 'somewhere' and possessed by some individuals.

I have brought in the case of Buddhism because I believe that a lot of Western misreadings of it show very clearly what sort of illusions of peace we often work with. It is true that Buddhism's absolute is something defined wholly in terms of negation and absence, a state of utter motionless emptiness. But our temptation is to confuse this austere conception with the kind of 'rest' we normally experience. I act busily and tiringly, then stop for a period, and consciously enjoy my rest. This is a state in which I do not have to choose or act, in which obligations and responsibilities are lifted from my overburdened shoulders; and it is most appealing to think of such a state continuing indefinitely. The timeless calm, the serene half-smile, of the meditating Buddha look to us very like such a state prolonged and made habitual.

But nirvana is not to be enjoyed: because it is the end of the busy, greedy self and the curious and ingenious mind, there is no one there to enjoy it. It is real and final death (and nothing could show more plainly how little we are prepared to face death than the indulgent language of rest and sleep we so often use about it); and so it cannot satisfy our unhappy longing for a comfortable repose. I believe that, in fact, the *nirvana* idea has a lot to say about authentic peace, but we shall come back to that later. The point here is that the peace we are often interested in is essentially a state of passivity: peace means *not acting,* not having to choose or involve myself. And this links up with what we examined in the first chapter, the eagerness so many people feel to shed responsibility.

Those who criticize peace movements and disarmament campaigns often make the charge that they are actually seeking to deny responsibility in just this way. The search for peace is a search for purity and security without any readiness to accept that there might be a price — even a moral price — to pay for security; it is a passion to keep one's hands clean, to avoid the possibility of guilt and the hard and inevitably compromising choices of practical politics. Now I believe that this is a gross and dangerously perverse interpretation of the deepest motives of the peace movements; I have tried to indicate already how I believe the real irresponsibility, the real obsession with purity and security, and the real refusal of guilt lies with those caught up in the 'war game'. But for all that, this is a serious criticism and not completely irrelevant to some kinds of talk about peace.

When, in the late sixties and early seventies, 'peace' became so much a catchword and a slogan among European and (even more) American youth movements, it came as part of a package which included a deep suspicion of public life and social planning, an idealization of small, intensely interrelating groups, and what might best be summed up as a disbelief in original sin — a conviction that humanity could be drastically reconstructed by good will or love, a certain denial of history and guilt. 'Give Peace a Chance' was the cry of a sub-culture apparently persuaded that peace was a natural state of organic harmony between human beings which would 'happen' when once the obstacles of hostility and suspicion had been overcome. There is more than a hint here of the idea that peace is what is left when social constraint and its resultant tensions and self-doubts have all vanished — so that peace appears in rather negative terms. Unjustly so: there is also some sense of peace as a mutually enriching harmony. But overall it is difficult to deny that this represented a limited and in many ways naïve understanding of peace, even a sentimental one. It was a view which opposed peace to history. Peace was seen rather as a sinking back to *natural* harmony, an escape from the over-complex world of large-scale political decisions and from the obligations of assessing the effects of personal history (what sort of capacities and limitations have been formed in me by my past experience?) and social development (how am I involved in the wider structures of society?).

Against this sort of attitude, the accusations of disengagement and irresponsibility have some real weight. Peace seen as escape or release is not an ideal easily communicated to those who are bitterly aware of their involvement, like it or not, in a world of interrelations. In our present context, as we have already seen, there is a longing for the sense of innocence; and if one aspect of this is (as suggested in the first chapter) an eagerness to disclaim responsibility for the public violence of international politics, another is certainly the rhetoric of peace as a 'natural' state of human relations, which is there for us to slip into once we relinquish superficial feelings of aggression and memories of the violent past.

The cause of peace is not much served, I believe, by insisting that violence is an unnatural aberration. It isn't necessary, of course, to run to the opposite extreme of emphasizing the innate aggressiveness of human beings in such a way as to rationalize violence as an entirely natural thing, quite beyond moral criticism. But we do live in an extremely delicate situation, looking for an elusive balance: we are receivers and dependants in all sorts of ways, we have no choice but to be receptive towards the world and others; yet our distinctive humanness depends on responding and modifying what is given us — asserting a unique point of view, a self, that needs to give and express itself and define its place in the world. It is really a rather silly question to ask whether we are 'basically' passive or aggressive: the truth is that we all experience ourselves as both receivers and givers. We 'open' ourselves to the world and others, but we also need self-definition, boundaries. We have to discover our particular place, our identity, in interaction with others — which always involves a refusal to be swallowed up by others, and so therefore a degree of self-assertion, even aggression. Without this we impoverish both ourselves and the human world — remember what was said in the last chapter about the need for all possible 'images of Christ' in humanity to be uncovered and realized.

But such is the variety and — increasingly — the uncontrollable rate of developing impressions and stimuli that it is easy to feel it not as nourishment but as assault; and here assertion slips into violence — the 'defensive pre-emptive strike: attack before I am attacked; make sure I do not lose control. And the elusive balance is that between patient receptivity and responsible, creative acting. Discussions about the naturalness or unnaturalness of violence simply ignore the intricacy, the delicacy, of the individual's growing processes in a human group.

So there is a model of peace which is regressive, a longing for what is really an infantile condition: nothing happens and there is nothing to do. There are never any decisions to make, because the world is not perceived as a place where clashes of principles or desires or goals occur. This is indeed another variety of the social diseases we have already looked at: and it is not surprising that, throughout the history of our civilization (and of others too), periods of social and political degeneracy have seen the rise of movements that can be called regressive in this sense — washing their hands of memories and compromises to recreate a state of nature, turning their backs on history and politics.

And also, very significantly, turning their backs on *language*. The way we use language is a very clear sign of how we are all givers and receivers. We are born into it, yet it is an inheritance that means nothing — literally — until we react to what is given and begin to experiment with it. If we simply reproduce what is given, the result is not really language in its full sense: parrots 'talk'; but it would be odd to say that they *use language* or that we converse with them. And we measure children's growth in intelligence not by accuracy in repetition, despite the impression given by most of our present examination systems, but by skill in producing what are for them new combinations of words and ideas.

Now the decline of language into formalism, inarticulacy or incomprehensibility must be seen in this connection as part of the flight from history and responsibility. When, in the language of the 'alternative society' groups of the sixties and seventies, we find an increasing looseness of expression, repetitiousness, reliance on formulas and passive unwillingness to argue, we are witnessing human speech in decay. There is a withdrawal from the risks of dialogue, of developing thoughts and images in contact with the speech of other people — part of the whole process of withdrawing from decisions and boundary-making, and so part of the refusal to be a self, an active participant in a group, giving as well as receiving. The way the very word 'peace' came to be used in some circles is a painful illustration of this. I have mentioned the song, *Give Peace a Chance:* no one could doubt its passion and its sincerity; but its deliberate interminable repetition intensified the suspicion of many that 'peace' was bound up with mindless, would-be innocence. Unintelligent passion and sincerity is not a very reliable tool in persuasion or transformation.

The trouble with a retreat from dialogue into the impregnable castle of cliché and repetition is that it encourages just the same process in those who might have been partners in dialogue. Idle and shapeless talk about peace helps indirectly in the creation of a language of war which is equally beyond criticism or discussion, and becomes a distinctive dialect of the impenetrable bureaucratic nonsense so characteristic of our century. Thomas Merton, in a brilliant essay on 'War and the Crisis of Language' (reprinted in *On Peace*, Mowbrays, 1976), demonstrates how the sinister and unreal jargon of war reflects the same hankering after 'final solutions' that underlies

the whole mentality of the arms race. He quotes (p. 142) the remark of a US major in Vietnam in 1968, who said of a military
operation: 'It became necessary to destroy the town in order to
save it.' Merton comments: 'The symbol of this perfect finality
is the circle. An argument turns upon itself, and the beginning
and end get lost: it just goes round and round its own circum-
ference.' The terms of an operation, the goals of a military effort, are defined entirely by one limited group: into their rigid
speech categories are fitted the needs and responses of all
other parties involved. Thus there can never be any need for
justification, and there is no possibility of assimilating criticism. Two dreamers wander past each other in the night, one
murmuring 'Peace, peace', the other mechanically repeating
'neutral' official records of atrocity: two comfortably self-
sufficient and final languages.

Merton makes some sharp and telling points about the
sudden burst of charismatic phenomena in the American
South at the time of the early civil rights demonstrations, the
Cuba crisis and the beginnings of American involvement in
Vietnam: 'At a time when the churches were at last becoming
uneasily aware of a grave responsibility to *say something* about
civil rights and nuclear war, the ones who could be least expected to be articulate on such subjects (and who often had
solid dogmatic prejudices that foreclosed all discussion) began
to cry out in unknown tongues . . . One thing is quite evident
about this phenomenon. He who speaks in an unknown
tongue can safely speak without fear of contradiction. His utterance . . . forecloses all dialogue' (p. 140). It would be foolish
to make this the basis of an accusation of irresponsibility
against the modern charismatic movement in its entirety, of

course: Merton is dealing only with a particular manifestation. But he does implicitly raise the question of how far some sorts of charismatic speech and behaviour can be signs of withdrawal and regression in a context of acute conflict. This is another setting, in fact, in which the word 'peace' itself plays an important and rather ambiguous role, and in which there can be a reduction of language to formulae expecting stock responses (this is undeniably the job of certain sorts of chorus). It is simply one more example of retreat and regression. And — as all serious charismatic theologians would be the first to recognize — it has little to do with the more challenging and more biblical idea of the Spirit of God being given to equip the believer for trial, and indeed 'warfare'.

The flight from dialogue into self-justifying, self-perpetuating jargon is, then, an aspect, and a very significant one, of a flight from adulthood, relationship, decision and creativity. To speak to another is to commit yourself, and to that extent define and limit yourself; but only in that kind of decision is creation, innovation, and thus human enrichment possible. There is a miserable link between militarized politics, consumer society, the corruption and decline of the arts and the cheapening and trivializing of language — in politics, journalism, advertising and worship. Fear of responsibility leads to the fantasies of popular fiction we explored in the first chapter, to the fantasies of destructive final solutions and the ultimate tidiness of suicide discussed in the second chapter; and to the regressive desire for a life without conflict and dialogue, the peace of the womb. Our inbuilt fears and our bewilderment in the face of a more and more complicated world make possible a pattern of political and international relations which pretends to meet these fears and puzzlements, but in fact collides with them and deepens them. This is the vicious circle of the 'developed' world today.

When dialogue decays, so does language. And when language decays, possible views of the world disappear. Language becomes a commodity passively received, manufactured elsewhere, so that the view of the manufacturer prevails. '*Most people do not or will not think round and beyond the language they consume, or maybe have not acquired the skill to do so. So they use whatever words and phrases they are given. The words and grammar of a language can codify a view of the world (including a view of nuclear arms), and . . . the language itself confirms, reinforces or even directs people's attitudes and beliefs*' (Paul Chilton, in the CND magazine *Sanity* for October-November, 1981). And to criticize and protest against a manufactured, official language which mutes the realities of pain, death and social collapse involved in modern full-scale war, we need a language that is itself alive and alert, self-critical, capable of argument, exchange, and, above all, imagination — not a bland and self-indulgent counter-jargon. The task of the critic is to prevent a shrinking of possible views of the world, to resist any tendency to fix the limits of what can be thought. And so any healthy peace movement will be vigorously productive of songs and stories: it will communicate a sense of alertness to the oddities and diversities of the world — part of the dimension of contemplative delight touched on in the last chapter. Above all, it will not suggest a picture of peace as withdrawal, mindlessness or empty leisure. Nor will it pretend that reconciliation is something which will simply 'occur' when various obstacles have been removed.

'Reconciliation' is a seductive word: we pray regularly for reconciliation in local and international conflict, industrial disputes, church controversies. But it is an open question whether what we concretely hope for is anything very near the reconciliation of which the New Testament speaks, whether the short-lived settlements brokered in these cases are more than vulnerable and unenthusiastic compromises. Professionals talk increasingly of 'conciliation' processes in disputes of various kinds (marriages in crisis, employment issues) — a much more modest word, suggesting, accurately enough, that the job to be done is really one of placating anger and pride, toning hostility down to a pitch of mere sullenness. Conciliation is only an episode in a continuing battle. To speak of reconciliation, as we use the word in talking of personal relations, or even of our relations with God, normally suggests authentically fresh possibilities, new beginnings, not a temporary cease-fire in a situation that remains basically unchanged. To use 'reconciliation' in connection with our public and industrial life is really rather strange, so long as we do not in fact expect or work for a change of structures, and think only of a readjustment, an overcoming of disturbances.

There is an illuminating analogy (suggested to me by a friend in discussion of the problems of industrial society) in the way we often think of health as the absence of sickness, and healing simply as the restoration and maintenance of a *status quo*. Such a picture is not false but, standing alone, it is misleading. It is just as important to conceive of healing as a process continuing throughout life, moving towards wholeness, and so of health as this process working in and through the 'conflicts' of disease or malfunction. It is a lesson we are slowly learning where medicine is concerned: 'healing' means more than the expulsion of disturbing symptoms by external force, but is also a co-operative with an organism trying to find and constantly re-create an equilibrium in its functioning and responses. 'Healing' may thus involve new departures in the life of an organism, and it will always facilitate adaptability. There is no static ideal state to which things must be returned.

Certainly, both reconciliation and healing in the Christian context have been seen as involving innovation, not only renovation. When St. Ignatius of Antioch in a famous phrase referred to the Eucharist as the 'medicine of immortality', he obviously saw its healing power as a transforming one. And in the death of Jesus the reconciliation achieved between God and the world is preeminently a transformation, an expansion of horizons. We saw in the last chapter how Christian commitment absolutely refuses any 'freezing' of relationships, how penitence implies active change. Reconciliation, then, cannot be identified with conciliation and — in spite of frequent distortion — is not, for a Christian, a fundamentally conservative idea. If we pray for reconciliation in politics or industry we are — if we are theologically serious — praying for change and newness of life; not only changes of heart, but changes in the structure, the dramatic script, the concrete possibilities in relations.

Peace, health, reconciliation: all of them are images we are perennially tempted to see in passive, naturalistic, or static ways. All of them, in fact, can represent refusals of the world (even health, when fear of risking the stable mechanisms of a healthy organism cripples and immobilizes people); and when they are so, they subvert themselves. Because they are exclusive, limited states, defensive positions, they are always menaced from outside, by the flux going on around them, always being pressurized towards history — choice, commitment, movement. Thus they can be states subject to deeply ingrained anxiety which can be coped with only by more and more tactics of exclusion and withdrawal. And this in turn means a deeper isolation, being cut off from the world's flow of life: peace and health conceived like this eventually mean *death*, which is after all the ultimately stable condition. Yet, as we observed earlier, death is not to be sentimentalized into a long and comforting sleep, into womb-like cosiness; it is an ending and a void. Not, for the Christian, a hopeless void, but none the less the final blow to the self searching for security and gratification.

The search for peace and consolation for myself by increasing withdrawal and passivity in face of the world ends in the nonsensical situation of a self which only exists in the first place because it is part of a network of relations trying to survive in unrelatedness, which is impossible. I may try to buy peace at the cost of the world, speech, decision, action; but I shall find at the end of the day that I cannot hand over the world without handing over myself as well. I shall not be left to enjoy my sleep.

If we begin to understand this, the impossibility of peace existing in a human vacuum, we may see too the falsity or at least inadequacy of our projection onto certain men and women of an ideal of calm disengagement, peace without real and continuing cost. The popular concept of the peace of the cloister, like the glib misunderstandings of the Buddha's contemplation, is a damaging error — damaging to people who hold it, damaging to those onto whom it is projected. It encourages most of us to think of peace as something intrinsically separate from the hard and familiar world, something we cannot expect to see realized in most of the reality we know: and it demands the impossible from the cloister, increasing tenfold the real and heavy pressures of that life.

So, where politics and international relations are concerned, this idea of peace is one very congenial to those whose business is the arms industry, and those whose interest lies in perpetuating the 'frozen' confrontations of conventional politics. 'Peace' becomes a beautiful, compelling and quite irrelevant thing, a counter to be moved around in the game, to describe an ideal situation which — fortunately — has no chance of coming into being. Those who insist on it as a present imperative can safely be dismissed as naïve, or else relegated to the category of those who have attained personal fulfilment (good luck to them!) at the price of living in a cramped and unreal world. The problem is that we seem to be faced with two essentially static views — peace as a natural state of repose and inactivity or peace as a carefully maintained balance of essentially incompatible interests, peace as deadlock. So long as our ideas about peace are passive or static in this way, much of our discussion will be sterile. The task of the Church is, as always, less to prescribe policy solutions than to challenge the terms of the debate itself.

We are driven back again to the conclusion of the last chapter: God's peace has something to do with an acceptance of God's world in its complexity. Peace as passive repose is as much a refusal of contemplative love as is the nightmare of mutual terrorism. This may sound harsh to those who, for good reason, desire release or rest. Peace is attractive to many just because it promises solace, the lifting of burdens — 'There the wicked cease from troubling, and there the weary are at rest' (Job 3:17). But here we can only revert to the point made earlier: this is not a peace to be experienced, but the end of all experiences because it is the end of the self. Desiring peace of this kind is desiring death. It may be understandable, but it fails to give real weight to the purposiveness of human desire, awakened by a call and a prompting from beyond itself.

If we are indeed made as 'desirous' beings, drawn forward into growing and exploring by longing and hope, isolation and immobility cannot be intelligible human goals. And if peace is a proper human goal, it must be a peace different from the 'peace' of death. When the early monks went into the desert, longing for a repose free from the tumult of passion, no doubt there was an element of 'death-wish' in their search. Yet the goal as they saw it was the repose of communion with God, in which what had been removed were the barriers to active, 'reasonable' love. Their rest, their *hesychia,* was a state of sharing in God's activity, and so could and should involve an unconditional charity to others — 'dying to your neighbour', in the rather odd phrase of one of the Fathers of the Desert. The 'death' to be encountered here is the giving up of self-assertion, hostile and excluding judgement: the spiritual energy wasted, poured away, in resentment and censoriousness must be retrieved and woven into the concentrated simplicity of God-like love, the restored image of God in the soul.

This remains in important respects a static picture; but it is by no means as negative as it has often been represented to be. And it has little to do with a state of passive or regressive disengagement, sinking back to undifferentiated unity. It acknowledges the fact that we have histories, that we have to move away from primal repose and absorption, out of the womb into a world of movement and variety, and that if unity and peace are to be re-established, they will be radically different in kind from the restfulness of pre-conscious life in the womb. The ideal of the cloister is not as simple and consoling as it at first appears. Indeed, it may have something unexpectedly challenging to say to those outside. If the *Pax* which is the motto of the Benedictine family means more than a spiritual pillow for the weary wordly head, it may suggest a model for that peace which can be the object of authentically and actively human desire.

In the first instance, the monk of the fourth century imagined that he was going into his desert solitude for *battle*; and Benedict in his Rule still speaks of the monk's 'military service'. There is in this a protest against the peace of adjustment and accommodation, the 'quiet life' of Christians embedded in society. The really damaging disengagement is in those who are unwittingly in bondage to self-serving 'passion', and are thus incapable of free action and clear-sighted love of God or others (as opposed to the 'passionate' attachment which simply seeks to feed off God and others). The monk's separation from family and social ties is aimed at an overcoming of a far deeper and more serious separation, the isolation of egotism, which is the true cushion against reality. It is a release not from love and choice but from self-protection, an escape from escapism.

The late Dom Hubert van Zeller of Downside Abbey told the delightful story of a North Welsh convent where the garden gate had at some point in a chequered career been reversed — so that the side facing inwards now read 'Private' in large letters. The cloister was being warned to keep its distance from the privacy of the world. This reversal is no bad symbol of the necessary revisions in our understanding of peace. The 'world', the unregenerate, uncritical life of most human societies, is the place of private, isolated existence, fear of facing the cost of decision and involvement — haunted by the fantasy of 'peace'. Because it is already in a state of relative withdrawal, it finds it hard to imagine peace except as an intensified withdrawal; having begun to shrink from tension and struggle, its ideal of bliss is the total removal of conflict and all that stimulates it.

In contrast, the cloister abandons privacy for a solitude which forces people to confront their fear and evasiveness and so equips them for involvement by a stripping-down of the will. The point of the ascetic struggle against 'passion' is the development of an *unencumbered* will, free to unite and to cooperate with God's will, having shed the impulses to self-protection and self-gratification which limit and distort its horizon. So it is a lifestyle which at one level *invites* conflict, the conflict of which the rest of society is afraid, in order to allow a more truthful and courageous humanity to emerge. And the peace of the cloister lies in and through this particular battle.

It is probably obvious by now that the 'cloister' I have been talking about is not simply identical with the monastic institution (though the religious life remains an indispensable sign in a healthy Church of the seriousness of baptismal commitment). For we are *all* enjoined at baptism to be Christ's soldiers, and to join battle with untruth and fear. We are all as baptised believers to some extent committed to a distancing from any social order in which real engagement with others and mutual attention, giving and receiving, are under threat. And this means commitment to understanding and bringing to light the hidden springs of conflict and protesting about false peace and self-deception. God knows that the Church is as prone to self-deception as any group, humanly speaking, and that Christians have to beware of the temptation to adopt self-consciously the 'prophetic' role, when all this means is a fondness for generalised denunciations. And yes, I am well aware of the reproaches that can be made against a reflection like the present one in the light of this. But the Christian can only try to be open to that resource within the Church that is not simply a matter of human discernment or human resentment or human self-promotion: the mystery of Christ's truthfulness which brings each of us constantly to repentance.

So the believer is invited to 'choose life', though at the cost of the usual cushions and consolations for the individual — and the collective. The Christian Church is bound to be a protesting body; it will rightly ask of its members a degree of 'monastic' disengagement, a sustained willingness to step back into critical distance. It will ask for solitude — distance from the tight huddle of fear, where people cling together to feed each other's fantasies. It will ask for silence — distance from the decayed and corrupting language of self-justifying and self-perpetuating cliques. It will ask for contemplation — distance from the manipulations and distortions of a self incapable of opening up to others. And out of all this will flow community, speech and action, all that we normally think of as the opposites of solitude, silence and contemplation. It is a death embraced for the sake of life — not the world traded in for the security of the self, but the fearful self surrendered in order to rejoin the real world, the truth of God's creation.

All this is laid upon us at baptism. But it is not imposed from outside as an impersonal imperative. Baptism speaks of a new identity *given* us — the identity of a particular human person who redraws the boundaries of what it is to be human; The impulse and the resource for our new commitment to creative disengagement, death for the sake of life, lies in Jesus of Nazareth; and what we mean by speaking of 'Christ's peace' is what we shall be examining in the next chapter.

4 Not as the World Gives

When the Jesus of the fourth gospel proclaims to his disciples, 'Peace I leave with you; my peace I give to you, not as the world gives do I give to you' (John 14:27), the assurance most Christians tend to hear in these words is of a peace more secure and lasting than any the world can offer. But this is not precisely what is said: 'not as the world gives' suggests both that the peace in question is not of the same sort as anything we habitually call peace, and that the giving itself is of a new and different order. What is offered and the way it is offered are alike a challenge to the world's peace.

In all strands of the gospel tradition, Jesus is not a figure readily associated with peace in the sense of visible harmony. He provokes conflict and confrontation, and says truly enough that he brings not peace but a sword (Matthew 10:34), that he comes to kindle a fire on the earth (Luke 12:49). In response to him, men and women discover and decide the basic orientation of their thoughts and wants: they are *judged*, and thus they unearth in themselves all kinds of hidden divisions and disunities. It may be true to say that through Jesus the world can discover a fundamental unity, a community of destiny; but it would be a fatal reduction of the Gospel to say that Jesus's work is simply the revelation of universal brotherhood. As has so often been said, it is hard to understand why anyone purveying such a bland message should ever be crucified. To preach a *natural* unity between all human beings as something simply to be seen and acknowledged takes us back to the fantasies of a natural state of peace and passive 'interlocking' which we looked at in the previous chapter. Before human unity can mean anything, we need to see why it is not obvious — how situations have been created in which there is no community of interest and purpose between people. We need to grasp in penitence how we have co-operated in fragmenting a world called to unity. And this does not mean scraping away divisions and distinctions to find an equality 'under the skin', but committing ourselves *in* our diversity to the creation of new and mutually enriching patterns of interaction. If our historical actions have created a divided world, our historical actions, our choice and speech and imagination, must create a world of positive mutuality.

And this precipitates the new and grave division of which Jesus speaks so sombrely — the division between the penitent and the impenitent, between those who see the world's calling to community and those content with fragmentation. The tragic impasse is that those compelled by the vision of community are driven by this vision to rupture many of the forms of communal living they are already involved in, because the uncritical acceptance of these forms implies an acceptance of the corrupt and divisive wider structures of which they are a part — or simply because these forms cannot tolerate the presence within them of a wider vision. The New Testament is haunted by the breach with the synagogue; Paul in Romans struggles to see how this destructive and bitter schism can be a stage in the creation of a wider 'peace' in God's mercy. Jesus himself, in the passages already quoted, is poignantly aware of the threat to the treasured harmony of family life. To receive Christ's peace is to share Jesus's own position as a sign of contradiction, and to be drawn into a course of action that seems constantly to be deepening rather than healing the gulfs of understanding in the human world.

Can we somehow ease this dilemma by appealing to some gift of 'inner' peace which provides the resources for dealing with the confrontations of the world outside? Is Christ's peace not the peace, the authority and confidence, which characterized Jesus as a person? Certainly it is true that when we talk about Christ's peace we must mean some kind of share in Jesus's life or experience; but insofar as we can say anything with confidence about what kind of a man Jesus was, there seems at first little to reassure us. The gospels do not present us with a figure marked by any evident serenity — rather with someone in important respects scarred by his own divisive role and painfully aware of the costliness of what he is doing. He has to bear the knowledge that he will cause the destruction of the peace of Jerusalem (Luke 19:41-44); worse still, his calling of Judas turns out to be a call to catastrophe and despair, to self-damnation (Mark 14:21). He cannot spare men and women the effects of his presence; and he does not hold back his tears.

So he is a sign of contradiction not least because he is himself so vulnerable to the contradiction he provokes. The crisis, the dividedness, seems to run through his own person. Spiritually as well as materially, it seems that the Son of Man has no place to lay his head, but that he must carry in himself both the compulsion of his calling, the unanswerable command to be the Father's Son in all things and to force the Kingdom closer, and the cold clarity of knowing that his presence as the Son and the herald of the Kingdom is for some an occasion of sin and self-destruction. Without his presence, some might have lived and died in their innocence (John 15:22). He must sustain the urgent and transfiguring vision of an ultimate mercy at last made plain and the knowledge that he cannot make it so plain that all will see it. His irony, his imagination, his anger, his despair, his many-layered and even anarchic wit, all of them stem from the struggle to make visible to all what is to him so visible that it needs no description and escapes all description; and when he cries out against the obstinate stupidity of his hearers, it is because he has exhausted the resources of language and picture to no avail in trying to communicate to people what lies in front of their noses. He is at once eloquent and inarticulate; and at last, confronted with the rational politics of Caiaphas, he falls silent. 'If I tell you, you will not believe; and if I ask you, you will not answer' (Luke 22:67-68).

This is not peace as we see it. Jesus is a man profoundly not at home with his world and his contemporaries, and so in our terms a singularly unpeaceful person. And his isolation is not somehow smoothed over by a warming private conviction that all is well: his faith is a weightier and a darker thing than that. There is no peace for him on earth, in the present order. His life is directed towards the coming Kingdom — which is an order of peace quite different from the 'quiet life' we may long for. Jesus's miracles are often seen as 'signs of the Kingdom', clues to the fact that it is at the door; and they are miracles of freeing from bondage, healing, feeding, and life-giving. They speak of a realm where the Father's will is done by the removal of what actively damages and limits human dignity. And the recurring image of the Kingdom's joy is the feast of the royal Messiah, the king's banquet thrown open to paupers, cripples, rogues and vagabonds.

There is peace at the banquet not because nothing is happening but because people are reconciled, accepted sufficiently to relate to each other in love, gift and enjoyment. They are at home with each other and their host; they are at peace and they are *making* peace. But the food at the messianic feast, the supply of nourishment which makes it possible, is the love and welcome of the host. And when we in the present crisis, the moving world of time, anticipate the feast, we do so by remembering just how that love took final shape for us. Our food is the crucifixion: a body broken.

Yes, the Eucharist is the visionary sacrament of peace, the foretaste of the peaceful Kingdom of the Messiah. But the price of our sitting down in harmony is the echoing discord of the crucifixion, the memory of the unpeaceful end of an unpeaceful life. Our peace is only authentic, it seems, when the world's peace has been broken, exposed as false; when the passive consensus favoured by Caiaphas has been so upset that it brings out its latent violence against whatever disturbs it. Jesus's peace can only happen when such a crisis has been provoked. His own uneasiness, unpeacefulness, is a kind of persistent questioning: just how much of the truth can the world bear without arming itself? Can the world, the orderly society of occupied Palestine, 'contain' the announcement of a final compassion which confuses all barriers of purity and probity? Can this society be a *catholic* society? The answer is that it cannot contain such a vision. Jesus is, as Bonhoeffer put it, 'edged out' to the cross; Jesus's followers are likewise squeezed out of their religious milieu into a new community without the familiar barriers. The Church is what is expelled by societies as they struggle with the challenge of God's peace.

No social order is equipped to 'contain' this challenge: all are doomed to their varying degrees of defensiveness and dividedness, and the Church will always in our history be precipitated out. Perhaps the test of a society's health from the Christian point of view is how well it can continue to live with and listen to (not just tolerate) such a critical presence. For the Church, like its Lord, proclaims God's peace best when least preoccupied with maintaining a bland consensus with society, when it is most ready to be uneasy and constructively suspicious (and that is why it itself needs sometimes to 'precipitate' its own protest groups, like the monastic movement, as we noted in the previous chapter). It gathers around the Eucharistic table to hold together the present realities of struggle and breakage, and the hope of the Kingdom where we shall seriously, affirmingly and joyfully look each other in the face, at peace in Jerusalem. And again: we gather to recognize the way in which the struggle runs *through* us; in penitence, we look at our own refusals to be catholic, we bring to the surface our own resistance to grace. What we think of as the redeemed soul or mind or spirit is what is precipitated, drop by drop, in these regularly renewed confrontations with the defensive worldliness in each of us.

The trouble with all this is that it seems to make the present a time full of tension, and to reserve all genuine peace for the future. We are doomed to be so preoccupied with false peace, the tearing up of false treaties, the breaking up of deceptive harmonies, that the Church can come to sound like a strained revolutionary cell, in which present fulfilment is shunned for the sake of a rather vaguely imagined future. Irony, suspicion and dis-ease — the frame of mind we associate with figures like Kierkegaard — seem to bypass the joy and peace which Paul (Galatians 5:22) describes as the present fruit of the spirit. We have, of course, stressed that the Church exists to show in the form of its common life the final destiny of the human race; it gives a place and a value to all. But what about the mental and spiritual life of the individual? Is this doomed to a perpetual anxiety?

This is a difficult question. The anticipation of the Kingdom in the life of the Church can hardly be a corporate reality unless it is also, in some degree, an individually experienced one. The revolutionary totally incapable of achieving a revolution in his or her personal feeling and understanding is a very unhopeful sign of the possibilities of the new age. But a *complete* personal transformation in the present would seem to take us back to that denial of the pressures of history that we examined in the last chapter, the withdrawal into private comfort.

Wittgenstein said that the happy person and the unhappy person inhabit different worlds; and most of us know from experience that happiness can be a curiously exclusive thing. The couple happily in love may be full of concern and goodwill for the less happy, may want to draw others into their happiness; but, to the truly unhappy, they speak a foreign language. The more their fulfilment is manifest, the more cruel and un-bridgeable seems the gulf between them and the wretched, the tormented, the failed. A church which sets great store by tangible fulfilment, spiritual security, hopes satisfied, is bound to be like this — a warm little house on an enormous black moor, inside, warm and content, outside, weeping and loss, intensified by the very presence of the unattainable little haven.

And, of course, vice versa, unhappiness is just as hermetically sealed. We talk rather easily about the way Great Art, or something of the sort, can 'lift us out of ourselves'. But nothing is bitterer than to listen, say, to a transcendentally joyful and affirmative piece of music when you are in a deep-rooted depression or anxiety. Beauty is palpably *there;* but it does not make any difference (again and again returns, oppressively, the cliché of the officer in the extermination camp going home in the evenings to listen to Mozart). It does not have to transform anything, and it cannot console those out of its reach in time or space. The gospel of beauty (Dostoyevsky's famous — and often misinterpreted — saying that 'Beauty will save the world') is a bad candidate for the status of universal good news. Anyone seriously aware of the horrors of the world, past and present, can (and should) say that such a gospel on its own is trivial — if not indeed 'inaudible'. The unhappy person cannot hear it.

Two worlds, two languages; and, most basically, two sorts of human experience incommunicable to each other, but incapable of simply denying or destroying each other. In my wretchedness I may not be able to 'hear' or understand the

Christmas Oratorio; but I cannot say it does not exist, that the human roots of it are unreal. In my contentment, I may be deaf to the cries of Job (as his 'comforters' were), but I cannot deny the reality of misery before me. Humankind may not be able to bear very much reality; it certainly has problems in bearing, entering into, more than one reality at a time.

Is there then any 'peace' between these two worlds except a truce of mute incomprehension? We have seen that peace cannot mean a disengagement from the world's pain, a retreat into private and exclusive security. But equally it is not a fixed pessimism combined with an abstract future hope. Somehow it does exist *in* the world, in history, in the flesh; and if so, it must exist in the tension between the two worlds we have described — not in one alone, and not in the static co-existence of the two side by side, unaffected by each other.

This is where we must turn back to the figure of Jesus, and ask again what 'his' peace might mean. We can recognize that the peace of his Kingdom is an active love which upset the illusory peace of the present order; but what of *Jesus's* peace? He was an unpeaceful man in terms of the circumstances of his life and death, an unpeaceful man too in the sense that he evidently suffered from the constraints of his mission and its consequences. Is it only a kind of evasive or sentimental religiosity that comes to speak of peace in relation to his person — 'My peace I give you'?

The New Testament writers are not as a rule given to religious clichés where the person of Jesus is concerned, and they do not forget the irreducible elements of conflict in the experience of Jesus. Later theology unashamedly pressed the paradox: Jesus was in constant possession of the vision of God, as fully as any human being could possess it, even at the moment when his soul experienced utter dereliction. He 'saw' God as he cried, 'My God, my God, why hast thou forsaken me?' In him, it appears, the two worlds could co-exist. The seriousness of tragedy, the loss of Judas and Jerusalem, the torment of failure are pervasive; the vision of the Kingdom and the authoritative gift of love are no less so. His conflict and pain do not eat into his authority or diminish his assurance; nor is there any suggestion that the joy of the Kingdom blinds him to its cost or prompts him to retreat from present need and sickness. The one experience sharpens, deepens, the other.

Often, in the context of talking about the relation between religious vision and the needs of the world, people will refer to the transfiguration story of Mark, chapter 9, instantly followed as it is by the episode of the healing of an epileptic boy. Commentators have sometimes remarked upon what seems the clinical detachment of Jesus in verse 21, where, confronted with the spectacle of the boy in the throes of a seizure, Jesus pauses to ask, 'How long has he had this?' But the whole tenor of the story is far from clinical: Jesus is disturbed by the implication that this is a planned testcase, a symptom of doubt and curiosity, and accordingly refuses to react by 'automatically' mobilizing healing power. The boy and his father must emerge in their individuality, and the boy's condition must be seen as more than a passing phenomenon demanding a magical cure. How long? What is it really like? Are you and your son really *there*, do you have a story, a mind? Do you believe? And when the full suicidal destructiveness of the boy's condition is clear, and the honest hopelessness of the father is out in the open at last, Jesus acts.

Fanciful psychological exegesis is a temptation to be resisted. But Mark's narrative, with its laboured emphasis on the complexity and gravity of the situation, its refusal of formulaic brevity, is surely working towards the point that transfiguration not only fails to take away sickness and fear, but provides no way of avoiding or minimizing or generalizing them. Dramatically speaking, this is a Jesus grimly fascinated, almost obsessed, by the detail of what he sees; needing to see closely and without any softening. Perhaps this *would* be fanciful psychologizing. Yet it is not fanciful to see Mark making a deliberate and sharply outlined model of the Kingdom's tension with the world, and Jesus's awareness of it.

(And since 6th August has become Hiroshima Day as well as the Feast of the Transfiguration, this hardly needs to be elaborated. Suicidal, diabolic sickness still waits at the bottom of the mountain, though now there are more bodies to look at.)

Jesus transfigured, Jesus fresh from the glory of the timeless Kingdom, stands still to watch a single small incident of pain, mental and physical. The transfiguring clarity of the mountain top is here as well, picking out each detail with a new light. At the centre, Jesus stands still, in both landscapes; with Moses and Elijah, and with the epileptic youth. Where he stands is, not a middle ground, but a space where worlds overlap. In his life and person, he defines what it is for glory and misery to come together and interpret one another. The Kingdom conquers, but not by abolishing the memory of the world of human failure and distress; only by taking it into its life.

Jesus does not achieve a theoretical solution to the problem of how Kingdom and failure, future and present, hope and memory can be reconciled. He simply lives in both, the vividness of each, moment by moment, feeding the vividness of the other. He does so, the gospels suggest, because his life is given up, moment by moment, to his Father. Every moment and every experience is to be absorbed with utter seriousness — not in bland passivity, but taken, seen, probed and responded to. This is the 'obedience' of Jesus (never a very good word to describe this attitude of alert attention); and it is possible — so various bits of the New Testament suggest, and the fourth gospel argues explicitly — because he *sees* the Father. In the texture of all experience, joy, pain, vision, humiliation, Jesus acknowledges a single shaping love, drawing his life together into a single act of response. The world — or rather all the worlds, of grief and of hope — can be sensed as given, the material given us out of which to make a whole and many-faceted offering, a gift in return.

Jesus sees the Father, sees directly and unwaveringly, even in terror and death. The gospels do not give us any evidence for how he might have learned or grown into this perception, and all we can see is its unconditional presence. This sense of steady vision was almost certainly one of the things which prompted the conclusion that the life of Jesus was from its beginnings 'owned' by God and transparent to him — the conclusion gradually refined into a doctrine of incarnation. And however we may theorize about the process by which Jesus might have learned trust of this radical kind, the fact of it remains, manifest alike in authority and in vulnerability.

Trust: the conviction not that all will be instantly and visibly well, but that all experience *can* (though not 'must') affirm rather than destroy; an anchorage, a firm point, a still pivot. And this we might indeed call peace — the fact of recognizing an affirmative and immovable centre. Part of the experience of trust is to feel yourself to be the object of faithfulness: someone or something is dependable — and, in personal terms, that means that an option in your favour has been made and sustained. This is the Gospel, the revelation of God's identification with the 'well-being of the human world; a Gospel which can be proclaimed only by someone utterly absorbed in God's Yes to his creatures, so close to that universal and fundamental affirmation that he can be spoken of as God's word, image, child, and so on: 'All the promises of God find their yes in him' (2 Corinthians 1:20).

So in this light it is no empty formula to speak of Christ's peace. He is 'at peace' with the Father because he is aware that no experience can sever his anchorage in this root of his existence. He allows his life to be defined by what the Father gives, by the manifold and even tragic texture of history; but this is not a shape imposed from outside, because it calls out free response at every step. Out of the central solidity of seeing the Father and knowing his will, Jesus turns the same receptive and self-forgetting attention to all that lies around him. He is set free by his bond with the Father to feel the variety of human experience without defence, the violence of hope as well as the violence of suffering. When self is immersed in the affirming will of the Father, it does not need its customary protections. The fundamental peace is not a state of *feeling* as we normally think of it, but a fact of union, constantly apprehended in fresh and surprising ways, constantly looking for new embodiment as new situations arise. In this particular situation, what does it mean, practically, to be at one with the Father?

Not, indeed, a 'middle ground'. The worlds of future and present, hope and hopelessness meet in a perspective wider than the world itself. Jesus is a new world — a new creation — where earth and heaven, even hell and heaven, meet. His Gospel is not a generalization about the state of things, it does not say, like one fatuous modern formula, that 'the universe is fundamentally benevolent'. The Gospel is that Jesus's God is King, that the source of all things and the meaning of all things is what Jesus called *Abba;* that his reign is at hand, that the manifestation of beauty and significance in the world is always possible and always close; and so, that we can live now under the Kingdom, in readiness and hope, alert for the vision of the Father, without abandoning the world or trivializing our history.

Christ's peace, then, is given us as we are drawn into his world, as we enter his 'space'. When we hear the 'good news of peace', we do not comfortably relax in the confidence that a particularly tricky problem has been solved. On the contrary, we are invited to *live* in the world of Jesus — which means bearing, as he did, the tensions of knowing the full force both of hope and of grief. We can recall here, perhaps, what was said in our first chapter about the importance of learning again how to mourn, how to face without panic and flight the colossal damage done in our world to the dignity of men and women. We are free to face it, not because of any reassurance that it does not matter, not even because of any reassurance that God will make everything all right sooner or later, but because we are aware of ourselves and the whole world as objects of an infinite compassion which calls us to the same compassion and sustains us as we try to embody it. And, having seen how decisively in Jesus this faith can reconstruct the patterns of human relations and the forms of corporate life, we enter on the project of compassion, trusting in its re-creative power.

If Jesus creates a new world, embracing two diverse worlds of human experience, one helpful image for what he is doing is that of translation or interpretation. He does not allow either world to settle down in its own conventions, but interrupts it with worlds from elsewhere. Into the world of easy hope he brings the memory of hell; into the world of self-indulgent despair he brings the affirmation of love. Each world is extended and, as we have seen, intensified by the other; and preaching the Gospel may often be to challenge the settled stability of one world of experience by opening it up to the other — as in the story of Jesus, 'We piped for you and you would not dance. We wept and wailed and you would not mourn' (Matthew 11:17). Jesus consistently refuses to be drawn into the comforting uniformities of unquestioned collective emotions. Once again, he refuses to *belong,* but creates a world for others to belong in. His homelessness creates our home, a place for us to live.

And we can live at peace, in the Father's will. Jesus is homeless just because it is the Father's will that shapes his future, his possibilities, and not any earthly system; it is because he is at one with the Father, living in his peace, that he has no home elsewhere. When we are homeless as he was, ready to bear the world's tensions and challenge the world's peace, we receive his peace and his Father's.

It is indeed not the world's peace and not given as the

world's is given. The peace of consensus or of quietism is given or imparted by joining in an act of exclusion. Illusory and corrupt forms of peace rest on a decision to ignore or repress certain dimensions of experience. But Jesus 'leaves' his peace to the apostles on the night before he suffers, before he enters into the depth of the experience of death and glory together; and when he returns as risen, marked with his crucifixion wounds, he greets the apostles with, 'Peace be with you' (John 20:19 and 21). And his greeting is at once followed by the sending of the Eleven, as Jesus has been sent by the Father, and the giving of the Holy Spirit — which we have already learned, in John chapters 14–16, to associate with the renewing of the Church's critical and challenging nature, with the manifestation of truth and judgement and the unmasking of ignorance, deceit and evasion. This is a peace which does not exclude, but searches out the heart of things to embrace the dread and guilt which draw people away from truth — the peace of honest forgiveness.

So peace is given to Jesus's followers in the Easter event, the crisis of passion and resurrection which is the ultimate collision between truth and falsehood, life and death; and thus the giving of it is interlocked with the giving of the Spirit of truth. The Church is a community constituted in the Spirit who constantly recreates in its life the critical transaction of the cross: 'the last, the dread affray' is, by the Spirit's action, being refought daily and hourly in the Church's life and the believer's life. And it is here, in this battle, that the love, joy and peace of life in the Spirit are being daily and hourly brought to birth.

They are brought to birth because, in the struggle, we learn to experience grief, rejection, failure, without the paralysing fear of ultimate worthlessness. Our anchorage is in the strange peace of the cross and the empty grave — and so in the Father who brings Jesus to the cross and lifts him from his grave. Our peace lies in the God who is silent before our cries and protests, and yet does not desert or cease to create and call. Paul rightly speaks of a peace that 'passes all understanding' (Philippians 4:7). It leaves us inarticulate and even confused (and I have found it hard to write about with any clarity), because it is so evidently not a matter of comfort, solutions, repose. It is a rootedness in the place of Christ, the world of Christ, a deep reception of the truth that we are loved and affirmed — quite simply what a writer on 'The Inner Dynamics of Religion and Morality' called 'basic trust'.[1]

When the celebrated Christian songwriter Sydney Carter died in 2004, many of the obituaries recalled that one of the compositions for which he was best known was 'Lord of the Dance', new words for an old American Shaker melody. Correspondence in some newspapers made it clear that the words still caused upset or scandal. It was certainly something of an anthem for self-respecting liberal Christians in the sixties and seventies, and has a vigorous continuing life in school assemblies. But the central image of the eternal Word dancing through the process of creation and redemption has quite deep roots in Christian imagination. The second-century gnostic book, the *Acts of John*, shows Jesus before his passion

1. Donald Evans, *Struggle and Fulfilment*, Collins, London, 1980.

bidding the apostles dance around him in a ring; and from the same period comes Clement of Alexandria's description of the dance of the heavenly beings under the guidance of the Word. Other theologians use the same image, and it receives its loveliest expression in Dante's *Paradise*. More modestly — but still hauntingly — there is the mediaeval English carol:

Tomorrow shall be my dancing day;
I would my true love did so chance
To see the legend of my play,
To call my true love to my dance.
    Sing O, my love, my love, my love,
    This have I done for my true love.

But there have been those too who pointed out that the image and indeed the title, 'Lord of the Dance', belonged more in another religious tradition. *Nataraja*, the King of the Dance, is a major title and manifestation of Shiva, the Hindu deity. Anyone at all familiar with Indian art will know those countless figures of the four-armed god, dancing within a wheel of fire, one foot trampling on the dwarf who represents godless ignorance.

The Hindu analogue should not cause us too much anxiety. To recognise in dancing Shiva an echo of the 'dancing day' of the second person of the Trinity is not to attempt some synthesis of Christian and Hindu faith, simply to note how the Shiva image gives forceful expression to much of what the Christian wants to say about the eternal Word's involvement in the world. The dance of Shiva is above all an image speaking of trust and of peace in the midst of what seems a profoundly menacing and hurtful world. Shiva, notoriously, is the god who combines sharp contradictions in his person. He is the creator and the fount of blessings; in the Tamil literature of South India, he is spoken of as consumed with passionate love and longing for human beings and their salvation. And he is also the destructive principle; not an annihilator, but a power that dissolves all forms to remake them, only to dissolve them again. He is in a special sense the god of time and death: he dances in the cemeteries, on the burning-ground, covered in the ashes of the dead. He is that which *limits* all earthly things, yet also that which connects them to each other, makes all things live again in other forms. Not surprisingly, some contemporary physicists have found this image the best way of crystallizing their insights into the nature of energy, flowing, dissolving and reforming endlessly.[2]

All this is contained in the icon of Shiva's dance. One foot firmly on the dwarf's head, one swinging high and free; the upper right hand holding a tiny drum — the drum which, when struck, utters the primal sound that initiates creation — the upper left hand with a flame burning on it; the lower left hand facing the onlooker, palm outspread in the traditional gesture of peace. The whirlpool of reality has a still centre, the terrible God of instability and ceaseless motion points us to stillness and greets us in peace.

'Not as the world gives.' It may seem odd to go to India for an image of Christ's peace; but there can be few other icons which so remarkably embody the fusion of trust and tension in the Gospel. If we turn back from Shiva Nataraja to the cruci-

2. See especially F. Capra, *The Tao of Physics*, Collins, London, 1975.

fix, perhaps we shall be able to see more clearly how this can be itself an image of peace: here too, one hand holds the word of meaning, one hand holds the fire which questions all words and images. The contradiction is poised around a single axis, which in this case is the unique face of a human being — more than a cosmic symbol. Peace in contradiction is more than a truth about the energy of the universe. In Jesus of Nazareth, it has come to be an abiding dimension of mature, integral human-ness. The still centre is given to us as we give ourselves to this symbol, the cross of Christ, the tree of life, looking neither for escape nor for resolution, but only for a union with the will of the Father.

The cross is the culmination of Jesus's living-out of peace, not just because it is a symbol of the absorbing of violence without resistance and counter-violence (though that is important enough), but because it represents the total triumph in his life of 'the Father's will' — the constraint upon him of the deepest truth, the reality out of which he comes and which is closer to him than breathing. For him, passing through the cross is the final peace-making. It establishes in the world of men and women the truth of an affirmation and acceptance beyond all our destructiveness, untruth and pain, telling us that we may have a 'Father' also — that we may be trustingly surrendered to the source of our life and the life of all things, and receive into our minds and hearts the stillness of Jesus's offering of himself, the peace of the cross. It will not take away inner or outer conflict; on the contrary it will force us into conflict, into battle for the sake of the truth we have been given.

The 'violence' of peace-seeking and peace-making, about

which people sometimes talk rhetorically, can only be the tireless readiness to assail our own longings for un-Christlike peace, comfort and safety — and it has to be wary of the characteristic temptation to psychological violence against others, dealing with our powerlessness by forcing others into guilt. All true; but the cross adds that we are not to be afraid, when the time is ripe for witness that *will* polarize, force an attitude into the open. And this can be experienced as a kind of violence by those under pressure from it. India, the U.S.A., southern Africa have all witnessed disproportionate fury and hurt generated by nonviolent protest, not only an intensified conflict, but an increase in actual violent activity and feeling by some. Part of what this chapter is about is the need to *feel* the tragedy of this without retreating into a castle of moral superiority; we have to recognize that conflict means that change is beginning. Whether for better or worse depends (not absolutely, but to a significant degree, perhaps) on our willingness to stay and bear the cost. And to do that requires the anchorage of the cross: trust, rootedness, faith and faithfulness. How this is formed and deepened in the lifestyle of the Christian we shall see in the next chapter.

5 The Cost of Simplicity

Jesus's 'Blessed are the pure in heart' is — like all the beatitudes — all too easy to moralize. 'Purity', after all, has come to mean, in Christian usage, little more than a state of sexual innocence (certain delinquencies being described as 'sins against purity'), and 'purity of heart' will accordingly be taken as freedom from 'impure thoughts'. But for the Jews, the pure heart was above all the heart devoted to God without reserve, the heart of the person equipped to 'see God', to appear in his Temple, because of his or her integrity and single-mindedness, unswerving faithfulness. 'Who shall ascend the hill of the Lord? And who shall stand in his holy place? He who has clean hands and a pure heart, who does not lift up his soul to what is false, and does not swear deceitfully' (Psalm 24:3-4).

The pure in heart will see God: as the last chapter suggested, 'seeing the Father', the vision of a unifying love, drawing all experience together, is intimately related to directness and wholeness of response. Impurity of heart, which fails to see the Father, is the divided heart, incapable of giving itself without reserve. The impure heart qualifies its response with conditions, doubts, reservations, keeping its distance; it is incapable of that movement of supreme assent and desire which is love. Or again (thinking of the psalm quoted above): the impure heart is one prepared to settle for less than the truth, prepared to make do with the illusory peace of consensus and security. It is a heart which never wants anything enough to be intolerant of substitutes. Beneath its readiness to make do with less than reality is the fear of real desire. For real desire means the candid acknowledgement that I am incomplete and need something in order to be real myself. 'Impure' desire, on the other hand, assumes that I am solid and important: I take things to myself as my fancies suggest, as much as I want of this or that, so as to keep myself solid and steady. I *consume* things — to stop myself being consumed by real desire, which shows me my lack of solidity, my need to find and nourish my identity in and with others.

Real desire is about recognizing that I have no resting place: my home is what I must look for, eagerly, attentively, as I grow and journey. And — the Christian will add — my journey only 'ends' when it reaches God — and even then it does not come to a comfortable full stop because God is himself a region of unending new discovery and reappraisal and fresh vision. Pure desire is desire that longs to grow endlessly in knowledge of and rootedness in reality and truth. Impure desire desires to stop *having* to desire, to stop needing; it asks for a state where, finally, the ego can relax into self-sufficiency and does not have to go on stuffing bits and pieces of the world into itself in order to survive. Real desire can live with an unlimited horizon — which religious people call God — while unreal desire stumbles from moment to moment trying to gratify an immediate hunger, without accepting that 'hunger' is part of being human and so cannot be dealt with or under-stood by an endless succession of leak-plugging operations.

So the 'pure heart' relates also to the Mary and Martha story — Mary sees that *one thing* is necessary and directs her desire to that. It is not an allegory about action and contempla-tion, despite the long tradition of treating it thus, but a story about integrity and fragmentation — wanting one thing, and wanting all kinds of things. And thus it is also about how the self is understood, whether it is seen as being drawn into a magnetic centre, or seen as being the centre into which things are drawn. The question is, 'Does our desiring draw our life to-gether, or does it break it up into a mass of passing gratifica-tions?' Are we organized by some attracting force beyond our own selfhood, or does the self struggle to organize things around itself? In the latter case, we have in fact another mani-festation of the urge for adjusting reality to *my* needs, the long-ing for peace on *my* conditions — a state in which movement and response and interaction will no longer be demanded of me. We have seen already how this is in itself a self-defeating effort, productive of fear and anxiety, and is, in the wider con-text, a death-directed longing — whereas the former option, our 'organization' by what is outside us, suggests a process of steady and abiding growth, 'eternal life'.

Jesus blesses the pure in heart as he blesses the poor, those who have the freedom to grieve, the unassertive (a pity 'meek' is so hopelessly negative a term in our ears), those who are passionate for the equitable community of God's Kingdom, the compassionate and the makers of peace, as well as the pure in heart; and it is difficult to think about any one of these with-out seeing how they all reflect on and make sense of each other. Purity of heart involves and includes poverty, the poverty of wanting one thing and not being distracted by many. Poverty thus becomes a freedom from anxiety and the desperate effort to shore up the precarious ego with superficial gratifications. And in this sense too, poverty is a lowering of defences; it exposes the self once again to grief, the possibilities of recognizing loss, frustration and tragedy in one's own life and the lives of others. So it makes mourning possible, and pity. To know mourning and pity makes domineering self-assertion unthinkable. Sensitivity to the depth and presence of others in their vulnerability rules out the bitter and harsh struggle for power in which others are made to pay the price of our fears and insecurities. Thus, inevitably, this involves the passion for equity, for a society where rivalry and struggle for dominance have no chance to grow; they grow on the soil of fear, of being threatened — and where, in the 'Kingdom', all are assured of the fact that they are loved and valued by the King, they have no root to feed them. And so peace is made. The beatitudes of Jesus, it has often been said, are far less a set of moral injunctions than a sketch of God's world, of what the Kingdom might be like. Those who see God are called his children, inherit all things, these are the children of the Kingdom, and their lives are marked by poverty, integrity and compassion. Their fullest and best interpretation remains Jesus himself; what they spell out to us is the shape of life lived in the Kingdom, Christlike life. They suggest how we might be, as Jesus was, a sign, in the tortured and broken present, of the healing future — present citizens of the Kingdom.

Poverty begins the list. Nowhere else does Jesus suggest that material privation and misery is good in itself (he has hard words for those indifferent to the wretched of the earth), and we must assume that he is thinking back to the familiar Jewish image of Israel as 'the congregation of the poor' — those who devote themselves to obedience so deeply that they have no defence but God. The poverty to be learned is dedication and dependence: dedication to the will of God, dependence upon the steady and faithful love of God. To be poor requires faith: that is why the 'poverty' of the beatitudes can only fully appear as a response to the good news of accepting love.

But it is also a response to the revelation that this compassion belongs to the final order of things, to the mind of God, so that it involves a requirement. To be in tune with the truth of things means being in tune with compassion, and this is the supreme *need* for men and women. This is what the 'order of things' asks from us for the balance and maintaining of the world in its interdependence. As soon as poverty is abandoned, we become preoccupied with possession (and so with rivalry and mutual threat) — the world being drawn in towards the self. New vortices of power and attraction are set up, the balance of mutual gift vanishes.

To see poverty like this requires a total shift in our understanding of need. Generally, we think of need as something *we* have which demands satisfaction — needs to eat, sleep, be loved, be needed. This is all very well until we draw the conclusion that anything which demands satisfaction is a need, and thus an imperative. But if we can see the need in ourselves as part of the balance of some universal need, we are less likely to mistake the momentary want for the true need.

This is a theme which both art and religion have considered in depth for literally thousands of years. Deeply rooted in all Oriental philosophies, from early Hinduism to Mao's Marxism, is the vision of just order: *dharma* in Hindu and Buddhist thought, *tao* in China. It cannot be described in the abstract, only sensed and discovered in the interlocking web of life as it is lived. It has often been a static, even an oppressive idea, especially when allied to the caste systems of India; but modern interpreters of the traditions have seen the error of associating it with any given order of society here and now, and have recovered much of its prophetic, critical and creative potential. It is a social ideal, but more than that alone: it takes seriously the relation of social and spiritual, and speaks of the necessity for an inner assent to the mystery on which all created harmonies rest (*dharma* comes originally from the verb meaning 'to support' or 'uphold').

And when the Jews of the post-exilic period speculated (as in Proverbs, Job or the apocryphal Wisdom of Solomon) about an everlasting Wisdom side by side with God in the process of creation, representing right order and right relation, they were expressing a similar concern. Even more strikingly there were already those in Jesus's time who believed that the Law, the Torah, had existed before creation: the rules governing human interrelation were not simply invented as a convenience but express the mind of God. It is with this in mind that Paul can use of Jesus the language that some of his colleagues would have used of the Law. Jesus is the image, the expression of God's mind: in him the wisdom underlying all things has utter freedom to act, in all he says and does.

So it was a sound instinct which led Chinese Christians to

translate the opening of John's gospel, 'In the beginning was the *tao*', and to speak of the *tao* made flesh. In Jesus, the 'need' of things is made apparent: obliquely but unmistakably, the life and death of Jesus uncovers a pattern of sound relationships. He is a man who sees and answers this 'need', and so communicates its character and requirements to us; and in his resurrection, he returns to establish a community attentive to the need of things as manifest in him — attentive to *tao*, *dharma*, Torah, Sophia, and himself as the speaking embodiment of it. He is a poor man, never seeking to lure the world into the nets of his ego, but drawn by the wisdom that fills him towards the source of all, and drawing the world after him. Poor too in his defencelessness, his open-eyed exposure to mortal risk, because defence or retaliation would be a refusal of the need.

'Poverty' is the acceptance of being part of an interdependent order — being 'de-centred', in the language of another discipline. And thus poverty accepted and made one's own is, in practice, the testing and querying of supposed need in the context of a wider vision. Shakespeare's King Lear, challenged by his daughter to explain why he 'needs' a retinue of knightly attendants, burst out: 'O reason not the need! The basest beggars are in the poorest thing superfluous.' At this point in the play, menaced and desperate, Lear can only defend himself by a confused appeal to the 'need' for something over and above mere material sufficiency, and he seizes on clothing as an example. But later, faced with the isolated nakedness, material and mental, of 'Poor Tom', he collapses into madness: what he has to learn, on the 'wheel of fire' of his terrible humiliations, is the sense of a 'pattern of sound relations', justice and love.

They are not to be explained in utilitarian terms — indeed, they survive very poorly on this basis. But they are the real answer to Lear's anguished question about the 'need' for more than is physically necessary. What makes human life significant, more than animal? Not clothing, not the acquisition of coverings for the naked ego, but the conscious participation in an order of compassion — an order revealed only as Lear experiences Cordelia's free mercy and pity — and mutual gift. Lear is right to protest at Regan's brutal utilitarianism; but he only knows how to answer her charge when he has been forcibly driven into the depth of privation, when his angry, terrified, grasping selfhood has been shattered by rejection and insanity — a dramatic instance of harsh polarization as a preliminary to healing. His forced external poverty drives him to the loving 'poverty' of compassion and penitence. He has learned to die, because he has learned to be part of a created world resting on will and wisdom.

I have taken the language of a cosmic 'need' from Doris Lessing's remarkable sequence of fantasies under the general title of Canopus in Argos — 'science fiction' stories, in one obvious sense, but in fact searching explorations of the levels of the mind. 'Canopus' is a planet in an advanced stage of cultural, mental and spiritual maturity, engaged in the nurture and education of a large number of dependent planets (including one disastrously unsuccessful and vulnerable planet known as 'Shikasta', 'the broken or hurt one,' whose history will be painfully familiar to all terrestrial readers). The hope of Canopus is to forge and maintain a link with its dependencies enabling them to reach the same level of consciousness. This is regularly frustrated by the hostile, violent and destructively greedy planet, Shammat, whose aim is a kind of slave empire; but progress is also held up by the machinations of a third power, Sirius — technologically sophisticated, inclined to despise or suspect the enigmatic Canopus, proud of its skills, but hopelessly at a loss when faced with the complex problems of long-term planning, and psychic-emotional adjustment which Canopus understands uniquely.

The second of these books, *The Sirian Experiments,*[1] focuses on the tension between Canopus and Sirius, especially in their dealings with Shikasta, where both are conducting evolutionary experiments. Ambien, the Sirian 'heroine' of the book, is shown gradually moving towards some grasp of the rationale of Canopean strategy — quite incomprehensible to the Sirian technocratic and bureaucratic planners. She interrogates Klorathy, the Canopean envoy, on the reason for the presence together on one colonized planet (not Shikasta) of two dramatically different species: is one meant to be instructing the other?

> 'No, I told you', he said gently. 'They are a balance for each other. Together they make a whole.'
>
> *'In relation to what?'*
>
> As I said this I realized I had come out with a real question: one that he had been waiting for me to ask. At once he replied: 'In relation to *need.*'
>
> And my disappointment made me snap out: 'Need, need, need. You always say need. What need?'
>
> He did not reply. (p. 195)

1. Jonathan Cape, London, 1981.

Later in the book, Ambien discovers a private note, jotted down by another Canopean official with whom she has been arguing.

> How is it possible that an Empire (Sirius) can be so large, so strong, so long-lasting . . . and yet never have any inkling at all of the basic fact? . . . They let their populations rage out of control, and then suddenly limit them to practically nothing. And all this done according to a temporary balance of social forces and opinion — *never* according to Need. (p. 151)

The Sirians are unable to conceive of their function in relation to a whole, their place in a world, in an order; and so they are helpless in the face of questions of meaning, and essentially arbitrary, anxious and defensive, in their foreign and domestic policy. Their social life is uneven in its development and they are quite unable to avoid suspicious sectionalism; and their governing model in relations with other 'empires' is rivalry.

Sirius as a civilization is a myth of that level of awareness with which most of this book has been concerned. It is not openly and barbarously destructive, like Shammat, but its imbalances trap it in destructive patterns. And the basic imbalance is the development of technical and what could be called managerial skill in the absence of any parallel development of moral and spiritual sensitivity.

The result of such a disproportion is that there comes to be no way of evaluating technical development — so that it is instantly assumed that if a thing *can* be done it *must* be done. If a new technological refinement is seen to be theoretically possible, then it must be produced, regardless of cost, risk, or long-term consequences, and a market created. Of course all this is most obvious in the world of military technology. What fuels the arms race at least as much as national and international paranoia is the sheer energy and inventiveness of the armaments industry and its teams of researchers. Enormous profits are involved, so that there is heavy pressure on governments to invest in a spiral of technical development to which there is no obvious ceiling. President Eisenhower warned us, fifty years ago, about the growth of a 'military-industrial complex' which would effectively take over much of the decision-making from democratically elected governments: it was one of his most accurate forecasts. And (thinking back to the first chapter) it is alarming to think that the fatalism and impotence about the drift towards disaster felt by the average citizen is likely to be shared by governments.

But this is not the only area where 'need' is dramatically neglected, and development has been allowed to proceed uncriticized. Whatever the rights and wrongs of the growth of the nuclear energy industry, it is sadly undeniable that policy decisions have been made about its development in this and other countries which have bracketed or bypassed long-term questions about the social and economic effects of steady expansion (and now it appears that the major justification in terms of likely energy 'needs' in the future — i.e. maintaining present or higher levels of consumption — has been based on questionable calculations). Once again, the fact of spectacular technical advance has largely dictated choices: the question of appropriate alternative paths of research has barely been raised at administrative level.

We might think also of the phenomenal developments in micro-technology of recent decades: information storage on a huge scale in very small 'containers' has become unexceptional (I am writing on a laptop, which would have been an unusual luxury when I was drafting the first version of this book twenty years ago), and the Internet is now an unprecedented source of information — and misinformation — for all. There are at least three complex moral questions that have arisen in connection with this, each illustrating in different ways the problems of thinking about technology without a corresponding 'metaphysic' in which to locate science, information, research and so on. There is the messianism that surrounds the whole subject, as if the social and economic stresses of poorer nations could be resolved by the availability of improved information technology (IT); there are some foolish things said and written about technology in the classroom as a solution to shortages of teaching staff. Then there is the recurrent anxiety about the uncontrollable character of Internet and websites: children exposed to pornography, space given to political extremism, indeed, the general culture of extreme and abusive utterance prevailing in much electronic 'debate'. And finally, there is the deeper anxiety that comes from the awareness of expanded possibilities of surveillance. Even in a situation where we want to reinforce security and improve intelligence work, we have qualms about electronic supervision and real fears about the ready dissemination of personal information about individuals. The law makes serious attempts to police all this, but its success is bound to be limited.

What are the choices we can and should be making in this

area? To take just one example: it is certainly true that IT contributes immensely to education; to see students with laptops working with a teacher equipped with an interactive board at the front of a classroom is to see a wholly creative partnership between human contact and technological skill. Someone has discerned what task the technology has to do within a larger picture, instead of turning to technology as a substitute for the worst of work. It is that discernment (to use the word yet again) that we are required to find in so many other areas. And perhaps the most acute and difficult these days is the cluster of issues around genetic manipulation, from human cloning to the modification of crops. Here above all the questions arise of the wider horizon of what sort of human welfare is in view, and what are and are not acceptable costs — ecological costs in relation to genetically modified foods, costs around cloning in terms both of the use of slender research resources and of barely imagined ethical dilemmas.

The Industrial Revolution often (understandably) worked on the assumption that if a technique were possible it should be tried: the early nineteenth century was not an age much given to worry about long-term consequences, it seems, and we should not ignore or despise the exhilaration and dynamism of the period. But the growth of ecological concern in our century has shown in retrospect the disastrous results of a 'can = must' approach. What kind of ecological movement might be necessary or possible in the twenty-first century to rectify the possible long-term results of our new 'revolutions' is an uncomfortable question. But so long as technological issues and the discussion of the sort of human beings we want to be are kept so far apart, we shall still be a long way from what the Indian theologian, Metropolitan Paulos Gregorios, has called a 'science for sane societies'.[2]

As soon as these two areas are brought together, we are at once forced into discussion of needs and Need. And this will be a discussion picking up many of the matters already touched on: the kind of liberty we have and the kind of liberty we need, the sort of mutual and collaborative patterns of life which take 'the other' seriously, the *need* for a model of our use of the material world that is not simply dominating, but allows us to be and feel part of things, not detached and superior to the objects we use (let alone the persons we deal with). A Christian can bring to this discussion the doctrines and images of creation in and by Logos (Word, Wisdom, *tao*); of incarnation, the possibility of full but finite embodiment of Logos; of sacrifice, the surrender of assertion, manipulation, self-obsession; and of sacrament, the use of matter to enrich and transform human meaningfulness in relation to the all-embracing order of things.

Furthermore, such a contribution can help to reconstruct the notion of *desire* in the way suggested earlier in this chapter, and so to restore to human life and experience the sense of growth and pilgrimage, the proper suspicion of 'final solutions' and supposed utopias in the historical world — and also of policy based on gratification and passive consumerism. After all, what seems to result from both utopianism and capitalist consumerism is real material privation, both in sections of our own society and in the disadvantaged parts of the world. It may be bad enough that the vision of a video-culture of mass

2. Science for Sane Societies, Madras, 1981.

passivity represents a disastrous diminution of imagination and creative intelligence and responsibility; it is worse if we step back to see this static, individualistic and potentially total-itarian society against a global background of increasing eco-nomic inequality, over-population in some countries, ageing populations in others, and the spread of military governments in much of the Third World — no unlikely projection for the next thirty years. In that wider perspective, the comfortable consumerism we should like to see, the 'peaceful' society of passive, undemanding gratification at the hands of benevolent technocrats, appears pathetically unstable; and its very char-acter in such a world invites violence and hostility. Peace does not come without *integrity*, wholeness of human desire, which implies the reality of balance and mutuality in the world and so — as suggested already — carries with it the demand for compassion and poverty. In the terms of our second chapter, it involves *contemplation*, which is the way in which the convic-tion of the non-centrality of my ego finds expression in rela-tion to others, to the material world, and to God. It is, most simply 'purity of heart' in the world of relationships, so that "'they make a whole". "In relation to what?" . . . "In relation to *need*"'.

Thus the demand for 'poverty' or simplicity in the lifestyle of the Christian is inseparable from the vocation to peace-making. The beatitudes are all about 'making a whole' of our world of relationships, in relation to an order of balanced mu-tuality and growth in and with one another. So campaigning for peace is, in the long run, inseparable from resistance to what I have called 'passive consumerism', to the cheapening and trivializing of desire. And it is in this context, incidentally, that I believe Christian criticisms of pornography should be understood: the question we should ask about alleged pornography is not about its 'explicitness' but about its collusion with neurotic, self-protective and violent fantasy, the various forms of rejection of the world and of the other. Its problem is not eroticism, but that it is not erotic enough — not concerned with desire in its central human significance. And we should also pay attention to the critiques of pornography offered by writers in the women's movement: it is worth noting that at least one such writer[3] has persuasively interpreted pornography in terms of a fundamental rejection of nature. Women (and other 'inferior' beings such as blacks) have projected onto them a myth of pure 'naturalness', which the male mind both idealizes and struggles to master.

Simplicity, like peace itself, is not a straightforward matter of removing a superfluous top layer to recover a basis of unproblematic goodness. And it is certainly not a process of exclusion and diminution, boiling down consciousness or culture to a bare minimum. Eliot's famous phrase, 'A condition of complete simplicity, costing not less than everything', is easily misunderstood. Eliot does not say, 'costing a very great deal': we are not talking about reductions at all, but about conversion; not about suffering-in-a-good-cause, but about *death*. The simplicity we have been looking at in this chapter is that integrity of desire, purity of heart, which draws together and

3. Susan Griffin, *Pornography and Silence*, New York and London, 1981.

takes up the fragments of meaning and longing in us, and, so far from ignoring them or peeling them off, welds them into one act. And that is an act of 'dying' because it involves the final confession of non-self-sufficiency. It is not that we are left with a drastically shrunken self, but that self itself — as we normally think of it — is laid aside: the self as central actor in a satisfying drama, the self as consumer of power-bestowing knowledge, the self as master. It is precisely because suffering is so readily mistaken for death that we see the phenomenon of the person who lives a consciously 'self-sacrificing' life, yet seems fundamentally self-preoccupied — hard or flippant or vain or deeply self-pitying or sentimental: they are all ways of enjoying suffering without facing death.

These are the really shrunken selves. The vigour and assertiveness, the resourceful energy, of the manifestly selfish man or woman are much easier to deal with. But when the basic greed of the ego is stripped down to the morbid self-consciousness of the would-be sacrificial personality, the disease is in fact more clearly visible, the little dramas of gratification more poignant and more destructive.

Simplicity cannot mean this. Its opposite is not rich variety but clutter, fussiness and anxiety. Simple life is life in which we are capable of doing what we do whole-heartedly, which means questioning all those things that cannot be done whole-heartedly because they cannot be seen as parts of a whole 'in relation to need'. I have mentioned some of those aspects of our public life, political and cultural, which invite such questions; obviously the challenge extends to the habits and assumptions of each individual. We need an 'ecological' concern not only for our society and its public behaviour but for our inner life too — an ecology and economy of taste, emotion, sensation. Naturally, this is always in danger of slipping into the disagreeable radical puritanism (and radical pharisaism) which dictates lists of socially-approved habits and leisure activities and so on; and so it is important to keep a slightly sardonic eye on this tendency — remembering the risks of a search for *static* purity or natural innocence and the inevitability of compromises in a compromised society.

Perhaps the things we need to be most alert to (even more, maybe, than to the exact number of commercially produced sausages we eat in a week?) have to do with the response we feel to any invitation from society or the media to easy and unreflective emotions. Mass entertainment often invites us to self-indulgent emotion or easy mockery or satisfaction with cliché. Even the language of 'responsible' journalism often invites the same kind of thing. The great German Marxist critic, Walter Benjamin, wrote in the 1920s that our society was getting to be dominated by the idea of film as the norm of art and communication — the succession of 'shocks', apparently self-contained instants of presentation assaulting your awareness. It is an accurate forecast of what is normally thought of as 'news' today.

So when I speak of 'ecology and economy of taste', I am not recommending any kind of fastidiousness (which would be another form of anxiety). What I have in mind is a degree of discrimination — an active, not a passive, response to communication. Only with a discriminating, questioning response can communication turn into dialogue, and *move*. These are matters touched on a little in the third chapter: the renewal of language we thought about there is in fact one more aspect of our integrity as adult human beings, our simplicity, our willingness to belong to a collaborating and critical whole.

Although it may sound odd to associate the ideas of peace and concentration these last reflections may perhaps suggest why they might belong together. The artist or craftsman at work can show a kind of peace — a lack of restless distractedness and greed for diverting sensation; it is a peace of absorption and self-forgetting, and therefore not a privately enjoyed sense of repose. It is a peace which is part of response to a given world, engagement and — we may as well say it — love; neither passive nor frantically busy, but committed, and defined by 'need', by the form of the object. Something like this is necessary in the 'art' of significant speech, too. The good confessor, counsellor, or therapist knows that the task is to allow the other to articulate his or her identity and need through one's own attention. You as counsellor are there to learn the inner shape, the grammar, of someone else's mind and imagination so as to enable them to say what they need to say when they see this shape reflected in your presence and response. Again, a peace which is far from passive, but which seeks not to intrude egocentric anxiety upon the world — represented by client or penitent — and where one's own speech and experience are offered not as an imposition but as a gift to the self-interpreting of another. Listening for the *tao*, perhaps.

Sculptors speak of the effort to see what shape is forming itself in the stone, poets of discovering what their language wants to say through them. Odd expressions, but they show very plainly the quality of committed attention we have been considering. And the artist capable of such attention is capable too of embodying it in what is produced — in the balance, the sense of 'inner necessity', which make certain works of art so extraordinary. The contemplative explorations of theme in Bach's 'Cello Suites, the luminous autumnal depth of a Rembrandt portrait, Henry Moore's diverse treatment of the texture of different kinds of stone — these are obvious examples for many. And there are striking failures, too. David Jones is deservedly praised as one of the great letterists and watercolourists of the century, but it is possible to compare the clarity and lucency of many of the early water-colours (especially of coastal scenes) with one or two late canvases, in particular the 'Kensington Mass', where the load of symbolic allusion, barely contained in Jones's poetry, has led to impossible 'overworking' of a surface with detail. A kind of anxiety has taken over, reflective of Jones's tormented mental life: for him, the seeing of endless interlocking patterns of imagery was a positive burden, more and more inhibiting expression. Clarity yields to a desire to say more than can be said — to say, rather than to show?

The Chinese calligrapher, and still more the Zen poet or draughtsman, will wait until the mind is clear and void before executing his work, in rapid and economical strokes. In this way what appears is the fruit of a genuine concentration, a *centring* of the whole person, so that a simple line or phrase can carry and suggest rich content, though not a content to be analysed or conceptualized. This is pre-eminently the art of 'poverty', in the sense intimated in this chapter, because it is an art of contemplation. Nothing could be further from the concentration of furrowed brow and anxious calculation; perhaps we should do better to talk about a state of *concentratedness*, though even that carries overtones of stressful mental effort.

The important thing is that, although it is maintained by discipline, it cannot be described as achievement or possession. It is in fact a further dimension of 'basic trust' — trust that our fragmentariness will indeed be welded into a unity of authentic desire when we yield enough to be addressed and drawn out by the objectivity of the world, both human and non-human. This is not to recommend some euphoric spirituality of pure spontaneity precisely because of the dark struggle involved for all of us in hearing such an address and 'dying' in answer to it. We have only the promise that it is death into the Kingdom — freedom for action in communion; and we have that promise in the realized image of Christian faith, Jesus slaughtered and raised, set loose in the world.

The cost of simplicity is indeed 'everything', nor is it for most of us a price paid once and finally, but an *askesis,* an exercise to be undertaken daily. Undertaken in small personal decisions against resentment, self-indulgence, cheap drama; in continuing discrimination as we look at our society. We can learn to live with *peace* rather than *ease,* uneasy at our social world and its illusions (especially as it works in us), yet un-anxious for our selves and our power. A myth and an ideal, only truly realized in the man we adore as Lord and God precisely because he lived and lives entirely from the still centre of God's wisdom, even when his heart and mind split on the rock of human dread and evasion. But it is that conflict, that collision, which releases the power of the Kingdom, making Jesus the shape and atmosphere of a new world. We enter it in the 'death' of our baptismal promise, and commit ourselves to battle; yet it is in itself a world of active peace because a world defined by those qualities we have been reflecting on: poverty, integrity, compassion.

There is a little fifteenth-century poem which might be taken as a summary of the advance from false peace to true — although its anonymous writer probably meant it to stand for the cyclic nature of human affairs. We go from ease to complacency, to aggressive assertion, defensive struggle, humiliation and — peace; the crucial turning point is perhaps what we do with the humiliation, and whether it can be a real occasion of unselfing. On that depends whether or not the last line simply takes us back to the start again.

> Pees maketh plente;
> Plente maketh pride;
> Pride maketh plee [litigation];
> Plee maketh povert;
> Povert maketh pees.[4]

4. No. 136 in *Mediaeval English Lyrics*, ed. R. T. Davies, Faber, London, 1963.

6 Innocence or Grace?

The whole of this book has been devoted to suggesting that peace is a matter more complex and interesting than we might sometimes suppose. We may begin with a simple sense that any systematic programme of killing other human beings is an appalling prospect; we may even begin with simple fear — for ourselves and for those we care for. Then comes the question of how and why such a situation would ever arise, assuming that any sane human being would feel much the same horror and much the same fear.

But then there is a choice between two very different responses, and the response we choose will tell us a lot about what picture of the human world we are ultimately working with. The first is based on the assumption that conflict is not only as a matter of fact unavoidable but somehow natural, in the grain of things. We are committed to rivalry as we are committed to breathing and eating. In such a world, the development of technology, especially military technology, will be a constantly contested thing; what *we* know is what *they* may learn but must not possess; when knowledge is shared, power is in danger of being diminished. The other's possession of some sort of knowledge is the incentive for us to acquire a counterbalance which is not accessible to them. This was the logic of the arms race in the Cold War era, but it is not restricted to this context. What persists is the sense that political power is always a zero-sum game; what one has is loss or threatened loss to the other. So the life that we share is something that can only be defended finally at the (real or planned) expense of the other. Peace is a situation in which rivalry is to some degree artificially contained — by a careful balance of threat, as in the Cold War, or by the claim to a monopoly of deterrent power, as in the 'New World Order' that succeeded. These strategies may seem to be opposed to each other, but both in fact share the same assumption: peace is about containing endemic violence by means of threat.

The second response will not necessarily dismiss all this as dangerous self-deceit, though it may be sceptical of some of the ways in which the story is told. It may admit that, in certain short-term views, containment of this kind is the most practical goal. But it will want to ask whether there is any future in notions of shared goals or goods. The peace process in Northern Ireland has, with agonising slowness and incompleteness, been moving for a decade and more towards something more than containment: towards a dimly apprehended sense of shared good — even if in practice it has sometimes seemed little more than an acknowledgement of the existing situation as an evil for everyone concerned. So if those who favour a response different from the one outlined above ask how we got into a situation where shared goods are invisible and rivalry predominates, they will want to start their answer a bit further back. Human beings are prone to collective fear and panic, as much as individual disturbance, and one way in which they collectively deal with this is to erect systems which console them by offering comprehensive accounts of their own behaviour and destiny, and whose absolute rightness can be turned into a reproach against all outside. These are — as proposed earlier in this book — designed to guarantee that we do not have to feel guilt for what is done to others. On this basis, it will appear entirely rational to build up systems of mutual threat: the other party is defined from the very start as destructive of our identity, so that we can survive only by threatening his. And because military technology does indeed advance with a sort of pure and unpolitical indifference to both sides, peacekeeping is always a re-adjustment at higher and higher levels. But because this means an inbuilt insecurity running through the whole business, fear and panic are *not* finally contained. They are liable to grow; and since they are not rational things, the likelihood of everyone making rational calculations about the cost of war at every stage is not high.

The first kind of reply in fact assumes two potentially contradictory things. It takes for granted that the situation of deadlock is absolutely 'given', incapable of being resolved — certainly not by any kind of dialogue. This is a deeply pessimistic, even fatalistic, assumption. On the other hand, it argues as if people, especially people in authority, were fundamentally reasonable; it appeals to civilized and enlightened self-interest, and this is a very optimistic calculation, which sets a high estimate on human freedom, human capacity to choose rationally between clear alternatives and to put these choices into effect. There is a good deal of rather questionable reasoning involved in the deployment of these ideas. It is perhaps most evident in current discussions of terrorism. It is painfully clear that simple deterrent violence is inadequate in the face of those for whom death is not a deterrent and may even be an incentive to certain courses of action: the suicide bomber has unsettled a good many versions of the argument. At the same time, this is taken by some to mean that the suicide bomber has no kind of political rationality or intelligible goals. Now, while there may well be a good many terrorists who are motivated primarily by hatred and the desire to overturn and destroy existing structures with no scheme to replace them with — and even some for whom anarchic violence is articulated as a short-term *goal* (as it seems to be for some of the anti-globalisation protesters of the period just before and after the millennium), this is not self-evident. The Palestinian suicide bomber, to take the most obvious example, has a goal, the establishment of a viable Palestinian state, and it is not helpful to speak as if this were not an intelligible aim. It does not (as I have already implied in an earlier chapter) make the actions involved any less appallingly wicked. But it means that our reaction to suicidal terror should not be one that either assumes its agents to be completely devoid of the power of thought or assumes that the power of thought is bound to calculate that certain physical risks are unacceptably high. It should rather be one that begins by asking about the particular kind of rationality that is at work; we may regard it as perverse and horrible (so it seems to me), but we gain nothing by refusing to reflect what is distinctive about it.

Those who make such a point will be accused sometimes of naïvety, sometimes of collusion or cowardice. But the charge of a lack of 'realism' is one that could be laid equally against some of those who simply use the language of a war against terror in a way that blends the idea of rational deterrence by violence with the rhetoric of battle against unreasoning hatred and destructiveness. The spiral of violence in the Holy Land might suggest that this confusion needs unmasking: rational deterrence of the usual kind doesn't work against those who are committed to seeking 'martyrdom'; but the seeking of death for the cause is not a mark of irrationalism, otherwise it would not be used — as it appallingly is — as a tool of some kind of policy. Just as in a lot of the Cold War debates, there is a strange mixture of fatalism and optimism — on the one hand, there is no point in trying to go below the surface of apparently unreasoning violence, and on the other, we shall devise strategies of deterrence that will intimidate the other side by causing them to reason that they cannot afford certain risks.

The mixture of fatalism and optimism is interesting — and not all that uncommon in immature socio-political mythologies (crude versions of Marxism, for instance). The past is not our fault, and we are not *personally* affected by it at any deep level; it is an external constraint, a brick wall built by nature and history around us. But we are independent and free within these outside walls. By careful, serious, objective reasoning, we can steer our way through the dangerous waters of, our given situation. We know the terrible errors of the past too well to repeat them: we inherit the problems of our predecessors, but not their fatal weaknesses. Thus the development of warfare technology (not only nuclear, but chemical and biological) to its extreme possible point can be interpreted as manifesting our superior awareness of the risks we run.

Knowing what we know, we are that much more free *not* to give way to violent impulse: we have made quite sure that we and our enemies will make no hasty decisions.

The second kind of response I have been trying to sketch, the one that doesn't assume that rivalry is the fundamental impulse in humanity, may at first sight look just as fatalistic. It works with a suspicion (at least) that the mere possession of weapons and techniques of intimidation wellnigh guarantees that they will be used; and that the self-destructive streak in men and women is magnetically compelling. Looking at past history, what grounds could we possibly have for feeling optimistic? We must limit our military resources because if we do not *decide* to do so nothing will prevent them expanding indefinitely. This approach is rather dubious about liberty and rationality; it even seems to want to limit the freedom of states to defend themselves. Does not this suggest just as gloomy and anxiety-generating a picture as the first option?

It may do: belief in the absolute inevitability of war, belief that we are compelled to repeat the errors of the past unless more or less forcibly restrained, is not a humane or constructive view of things, and the cause of peace is not much served by pressing this sort of case. But there is surely an important point here. We inherit limited capacities of judgement; no one begins rational life with a clean slate. Options are restricted by factors beyond our control (defenders of deterrence are right about that), but also our own responses are formed by factors beyond our control. We cannot depend on our — or anybody's — objectivity and clarity; at least, not when the life or death of millions is concerned.

This is not fatalism. It simply points out that there may be disasters which are genuinely *chosen* but not rationally chosen. No mysterious 'historical destiny' forces fingers onto buttons; but all sorts of pressures work on people's minds to persuade them that courses of action are reasonable and defensible. This is so obvious that it seems a waste of time to say it. It is something which affects every area of our lives, and something which philosophers, sociologists and psychologists have alerted us to more and more in the last century or so. The important point is, though, that we recognize (as I suggested in the first chapter) that we are *capable* of irrational, even self-destructive, violence — and it is not something which 'happens' to us, but something we *do*. It is true that we are pushed and moulded by inner and outer compulsions, but that does not make it less our act.

So what is being said is that a great deal of our activity is not as responsible — in the full sense — as we would want to think, although it is not at all unconscious or involuntary. We consciously act unreasonably — i.e. out of fear, anxiety, defensiveness. Now if we are able to use the idea of 'reasonable action' at all, we know what sort of things would count as unreasonable — we know a bit about actions prompted by fear, etc. But, in the case we are discussing, we refuse to raise the question of irrationality. Although we are aware of the human capacity for unreasonable destructiveness, we exempt ourselves — or ourselves as represented by our rulers.

This is where the optimism of some strategists becomes a culpable lack of realism, and our uncritical acceptance of this kind of argument likewise becomes culpable. As I tried to argue earlier, we *must* face the fact that successions of ill-thought-out, short-sighted choices, dictated by evasiveness or selfishness, add up to decisions to accept at least the possibility of total war. And we can hardly suppose that, from a certain point onwards, people will begin to take decisions in a quite different way. All our decision-making as human beings is vulnerable to self-deceit. When we have grasped that, it becomes impossible to believe in the stability of a balance of terror maintained by people who, like ourselves, do not invariably act from calculation and objective analysis.

We are liable to self-deceit; but part of what we mean by 'rational' living is that we live in communities where our decisions are open to criticism. We reason together with others. In social groups which put a high premium on avoiding self-deceit and remaining open to the truth, the processes of mutual criticism are carefully organized. Not only the international scientific and medical 'communities' (an interesting word to use of them in this context), but the world of the arts also have all built into their lives critical perspectives and procedures — not absolutely water-tight and authoritative, but at least serious in intent.

How do we generate a worldwide moral community in which there can be a degree of mutual accountability, in which states may expose their goals and ideals for critical scrutiny? Despite valiant efforts, the United Nations is not, or not yet or in the foreseeable future, the basis for such a community. The weakness of the structures of international law is manifest, and there are powerful nations that are very unwilling to sacrifice some aspects of absolute local sovereignty by accepting such an 'external' jurisdiction. But there are in fact embryonic moral communities that do cross boundaries in numerous informal ways. Medical and scientific groupings opposed to nuclear policy were a striking feature of the Cold War period. Campaigns against debt slavery have won support across frontiers also; and — for good and ill — there is undoubtedly an international anti-globalisation network, whose methods have raised their own kind of moral questions. To put it very generally, where there is a sense of the human vocation or destiny as more than a merely national or sectional affair, as involving issues about the compatibility and interdependence of human goods across nations and cultures, 'global moral communities' begin to take shape.

The Christian Church implicitly claims to be the most decisive and comprehensive such global moral community; not because it has a complete and detailed programme, because it is an embryo United Nations or a superior NGO, but because it claims to have been given awareness of certain basic facts about humanity — that it is created by God for the purpose of joyful collaboration, and that it has been given the possibility of release from the ingrained compulsions of rivalry and self-serving. The existence of the Church, as has often been said in these pages, demonstrates the possibility of a community whose uniting rationale is the exact opposite of the assumptions of rivalry and containment as basic human concerns with which this chapter began. It is in principle a moral community equipped to challenge national ethics when they become obsessed with the assumptions of rivalry and self-serving; it is charged with querying the passionate desire for *innocence* that pervades such a lot of talk on the international stage. It may be that one of the abiding tasks of the Church is to help nations and societies come to terms with a history that is not one of infallibility and injured righteousness.

So often, when national and partisan histories are challenged, the reaction is angry and wounded and defensive; and this springs from the fear that to accept a different version of the past would be to be left in the present with no ground for any feeling of corporate worth and significance. It has been said with some justice that the rewriting of British imperial history has played its part in undermining pride in Britain, so that attitudes to British national identity polarise between bigoted and unintelligent nationalism (and racism) on the one hand and a bland and historically illiterate multiculturalism on the other.

But to challenge a myth of benevolence and innocence is not to substitute a myth of evil or hypocrisy. In a group's history as in an individual's, recognising the 'shadow' is a mark of maturity. Human growth involves choices made and prices paid, often in ways that will not bear easy moral scrutiny; to see what has actually made you what you are involves owning that not all of it is a story of righteous advance or of blameless suffering and heroism. Churches have frequently got involved in myths of national victimhood or national virtue (both Ireland and England have been cases in point at different times in their history); to turn away from this is not only an advance in the really 'churchly' identity of a local church, it is an advance in the growing up of a society now able to accept its fallibility. Not every question is destructive; not every bit of 'demythologising' in this connection is a blow to corporate self-confidence or loyalty of the right kind.

The churches of Christ, then, need to be comparing notes on how they bring these challenges to bear, gently but insistently, in any environment where myths of innocence have taken hold. And they need also to be involved in whatever international structures there are that continue to keep open the possibility of critical interchange and moral community. To take a concrete example: the Security Council of the UN is a body whose moral authority has been severely compromised in a whole series of conflicts; yet its ideal is important. Can the churches help to prompt some rethinking here? A UN committee of reference on matters of intervention and international policing, which involved specified and carefully screened NGOs as well as governmental representation, would be a plausible and constructive element in the present acrimonious international environment; it would guarantee that non-national moral communities had an input into certain crises and struggles in the international scene. The information available to even the most sophisticated national intelligence services is not likely to be comprehensive enough to stand in no need of what a well resourced NGO can contribute. The advocacy of churches for something of this sort would be a specific instance of the Christian body of believers nurturing moral community on a wider stage.

And this is where all that I have said about the positive dimension of peace and its unity with a humane spirituality comes in. I have argued that we need to be quite clear about the human diminution involved in defensive and militarised societies, but also that we are capable of living out alternative styles of life, rooted in contemplation, receptivity, responsiveness to the Father. If we are to answer the charge of fatalism, we must live creatively, showing that suspicion and the self-critical questioning, even the penitence, that go with it are the doors to a wider vision. The distortions of unexamined selfishness are not simply and instantly done away with, but they are exposed to the steady attrition of self-forgetful discipline, in prayer and in action, combined with self-awareness nurtured by a community in which mutual questioning is possible. And the focus both for contemplation and self-examination is and remains the story of Jesus as incarnating the will and wisdom of God, and thus as embodied truth, transparent to the fundamental reality. Self-criticism does not depend on effort and human invention, it has a given point of reference. Penitence occurs in relation to, in the light of, Christ; suspicion and challenge arise from the clarity and discrimination which should be nourished in contemplation, the silent attention to Christ and his Father which gives us a centre of stillness. Above all, both our self-examination and our silence should open our eyes more and more to the need and pain of others and the reality of the human world's deprivation.

In this way, recognizing that we are already *in* a world of cause and effect and interaction does not in the least imply that we cannot see with some clarity where we are, or that we cannot make some judgements of our motivation. We are not entirely trapped, but we have learned enough realism to know our abiding vulnerability. The revelation of truth in Jesus both establishes our vulnerability — we grasp the force and depth of our self-protectiveness and liability to violence — *and* creates a centre of light against which we may judge ourselves and through which we may grow in discrimination. Thus Jesus is indeed *grace* as well as truth; and the community created by him is characterized by both things.

So instead of a bold but implicitly nonsensical mixture of pessimism and optimism, the Church proposes a sombre realism about our deceitfulness and passionate unreasonableness qualified by trust in the presence of truth within human history. The former vision becomes bearable, we can face it honestly, when (and only when) we are prepared to participate in a community of truthfulness. And that community is in turn bearable because at its centre and permeating its relationships is the conviction that truth can only be shown and spoken in compassion — attention to the other, respect for and delight in the other, and willingness also to receive loving attention in return. If Jesus were not selflessly loving, given up to the Father's creative purpose of fulfilled life for the world, he would not and could not show us truth. His obedience makes him 'transparent'; and because he is 'transparent', he communicates truth.

Without the community of grace and truth, charity and clarity, it is hard to see how our individual and collective fears can be dealt with. But of course it is not really enough to talk as though such a community already existed in any and every church group in the world. If we put the problem in these terms, it is plain that we have a great deal of work to do in making the Church more Church-like. What I have written about the Church's possibilities as a place for critical and sympathetic shared exploration among people of differing backgrounds and assumptions looks like either a utopian fantasy or a recommendation of a vaguely religious debating society. Can we see more clearly what sort of possibilities there really are in the Church as it exists?

Over the last two decades, there has been an extraordinary growth in international Christian networks of various sorts. One of the earliest to develop, and still one of the best-known, is that around the Taize Community in Burgundy, an ecumenical (but mostly Protestant) monastic community founded after the Second War. The enormous influence of this group on young people throughout Europe and beyond has continued through all the upheavals of global politics. More than one generation has come to identify itself with reference to what the name of Taize represents — a serious political concern, an eagerness to listen and learn across cultural boundaries, a sensitivity for certain styles in art and liturgy, traditional in expression but spare and contemporary in expression, a profoundly contemplative spirituality. People have spent longer or shorter periods living in some sort of association with the Community — sharing the life at Taize, being part of a 'travelling cell' group, going around local groups to animate discussion and keep contacts alive, or in one of the small and fluid groups living among the very poor in Asia, Africa or Latin America.

But the model has been echoed in other contexts. The Sant' Egidio Community based in Rome has offered a similar pattern of network involvement, without the same strictly monastic structure at the centre. Its work has diversified beyond simple care and practical support for the poor in the direction of serious and costly mediation and reconciliation work (in Mozambique, for example). The Focolare movement has concentrated more directly on personal discipline and growth, but with a strong mission focus and energy. The community of monks and sisters at Bose in Northern Italy has elements of

Taize in its style but a deeper commitment to theological education and spiritual formation in the traditions of Eastern as well as Western Christianity, combined with an acute and informed social commentary and a strong international concern. Most observers of the Christian scene in Europe would be bound to note these phenomena: as conventional regular church attendance flounders in most countries, the vigour of 'the movements', in both Protestant and Catholic environments, seems to grow.

How then does it relate to the ordinary life of the local church — can anything like this become part of our general experience of formal Christian commitment? Certainly there is in the average church a place for the development of groups for shared prayer — not only intercession but silence: perhaps simply making available either a church building or a room in a house for a substantial period during which silence is kept, and allowing people to drop in or out for as long as they need. Likewise, the recovery of an imaginative liturgy will depend quite a lot on the readiness of smaller groups to explore areas of tradition in relation to their needs, in an informal and supportive setting.

All this would be little more than a pietistic programme if it did not include the global concerns of places like Taize and Bose. Most people cannot afford 'sabbaticals' to experience the life of other nations and cultures; but it is surprising what can be achieved. The British movement 'Christians Aware' has for well over a decade been organising working parties and learning groups to visit churches in the developing world, which have attracted both young and not-so-young participants in a low-budget cross-cultural exposure. The arrival of email has opened up immense possibilities for contact: church schools in Britain have experimented successfully in building relations by this means with schools in situations of extreme deprivation or stress, and have been able to provide a concrete focus for local appeals and campaigns. It is not that difficult for a determined congregation to become part of a global moral community, and it is surprising how much human talent emerges when this is undertaken, talent that can be put at the service of both practical help and mutual understanding.

The Church in England is giving a lot of thought at the moment to new forms of church life, to flexible and not-so-local patterns and networks; it is a period of immense potential for the diversification and growth of Christian communities. But the perspectives we have just been considering need to be part of any picture of Christian renewal worth contemplating. New styles of Church life need global insight and understanding and commitment; just as they need roots in the struggle to grow in critical spirituality — poverty, integrity, compassion. And they need too the presence of more large-scale and flexible structures for meeting and exchange, like the Taize and Sant' Egidio networks. Perhaps also they need the stimulus of some quite new kinds of community. Metropolitan Paulos Gregorios concludes his excellent book *The Human Presence*[1] with a proposal for such an experiment.

> There is today an urgent need for an interdisciplinary, intercultural, interreligious community of mature, capable, charismatic people who will live together for five to ten

1. WCC, Geneva, 1978, pp. 100-103.

years in a place where, despite the difference of nationalities, they can:

(a) participate fully in the life and struggles of the community around them . . . ;

(b) evolve a way of life, a style of living in community, with simplicity and spontaneity, not averse to productive manual labour, not closed to the world outside, not afraid of poverty (preferably in the midst of a non-affluent society), not closed to the religious and cultural sensitivities of others in the community at large;

(c) engage in serious and informed study and reflection on the problems that confront humanity today . . . ; such reflection to lead to the creation of patterns of living, producing, and educating which can be copied by the world outside;

(d) embody a new spirituality — *askesis* — based on prayer, meditation, worship, and sacramental life; on loving service and unostentatious self-sacrifice; on humility and graciousness, on overcoming acquisitiveness and aggressiveness; on transparency to each other and to the transcendent.

This is a programme both ambitious and idealistic, and it remains to be seen whether anything similar is likely to be realized. But its importance, as the Metropolitan makes very clear in his further comments, lies in the way in which it integrates the search for an authentic spirituality not only with social and political alertness but with the quest for new technologies and the discussion of values in scientific work — attending to 'need', in its most comprehensive sense. Likewise, it views all these issues as inseparable from the development of small-scale patterns of corporate living in which fears and aggressions can be faced and worked through. If a community or communities like this came into being it would indeed — whatever its interreligious character — be a 'Church-like' phenomenon, suggesting models for the Christian future in particular as well as the human future in general.

A church which could depend upon and look to centres like this would be a far more effectively nourished body than one surviving only on a diet of hopes, statements, vaguely outlined visions (like this book). The challenge is there; let us hope that there will be Christian people, among others, to take it up.

This book has not tried to give authoritative answers to the problems presented daily in the newspapers. When the cry goes up, as it frequently does, for the Church and its leaders to offer 'moral leadership', the temptation to assume the mantle of an expert in all sorts of fields is a strong one, and I don't imagine, I'm afraid, that such a temptation has been successfully resisted throughout these pages. But the aim has been other than this. I have wanted to suggest some tools for diagnosing a few of the things that are, as I believe, wrong at the root of the way we state some of the questions of national welfare and international security in our public and private discourse, using one or two cues from popular culture to find a way into our pervasive anxieties. And I have also wanted to suggest how the Christian faith offers some resource for meeting these fears and for reinforcing resistance to those aspects of our culture that will maim and even kill us as human agents if they are left unchallenged.

My practical suggestions will on the whole look modest to a degree; but I am not at all sure that this is as much of a problem as some might think. Talking about the limited and local, after all, is not just a matter of practical convenience or injecting enthusiasm into the despairing or apathetic. Christians try to live with the paradox of a limited human story that potentially includes and makes sense of all our stories, and with the regular enacting of a symbol claimed to be abidingly transforming of the world. People who are familiar with the imagery of incarnation and eucharist should not find it impossible to believe in the significance of the local and particular human gesture. Not only is it given meaning — independently of instant visible 'success' — by those central pictures; there is also a trust, obscure but real, that the transforming of the world is actually happening when the absolute self-gift of God calls out and makes possible something of our own willingness for self-gift. To use a phrase which I owe originally to the Roman Catholic theologian Nicholas Lash, we need to be careful about plans to make all the difference and instead attend to the difference that can actually be made in a situation. The gesture, the signature on the petition, the email to a school in Uganda or a clinic in Colombia, is, like the eating of a piece of bread and the drinking of a sip of wine in the presence and power of Jesus Christ, a moment when we try to let peace work in us, locally and specifically: a moment of truce in a world of terror, and perhaps no more than that; but a difference all the same. And if a difference made in faith and openness to God, then also a sign of the future that God wants, and a promise of that future.

Points for Discussion

CHAPTER 1

Our own attitudes to violence in the media, or violence in our towns and neighbourhood — how far do these attitudes relate to what we think about war?

How much do we really believe we can make a difference to things — in society in general, in our places of work, in the church?

Are there individuals or groups of people whom we regard as unqualified enemies? How serious is our belief in a common humanity?

CHAPTER 2

Is it simply idealistic to expect 'repentance' to be part of political life?

Is it right to condemn at international level tactics (threat or terror) we should question at the private level? Or do international affairs demand different standards?

What sort of attitude is involved in 'contemplating' other people? How might the Church explore this and foster it in a community?

CHAPTER 3

How do we experience language being used by others to mould, or distort, our own reactions (in advertising, in the newspapers, at work, etc.)?

What, if anything, do we ask from people leading the monastic life? Are our expectations of them realistic?

Is it really possible to draw such clear distinctions between privacy and solitude? When we need to be alone, what are we looking for?

CHAPTER 4

Is it fair to talk about Jesus as a revolutionary? Or — on the opposite side — to talk about Jesus as a pacifist? How do we, and how should we, use the example of Jesus in assessing our contemporary calling?

How do we understand the idea of 'obedience to the will of God'?

In what sort of ways do feelings — positive or negative, happy or painful — affect our faith and trust?

CHAPTER 5

How are we affected by 'passive consumerism'? How do we react to advertising?

Where *should* decisions about 'technological developments be taken? Isn't there a case for saying that those with expertise should make the policies?

In what ways is 'need' a matter of more than material necessity or minimum conditions for survival? How should we talk about its spiritual or imaginative side?

CHAPTER 6

Why are peace movements seen as naïve? What ideas of human nature underlie appeals to 'realism' and are they Christian?

What opportunities are there locally for groups to discuss the question of peace? What practical steps might be taken in educating ourselves and others and widening our horizons?

Are 'symbolic gestures' worthwhile, and if so, why?